Immanuel Kant's Lectures on Psychology

Immanuel Kant

Immanuel Kant's Lectures on Psychology

*With an introduction
by Carl du Prel:
"Kant's mystical world view"*

Immanuel Kant

translated by Kerry A Nitz

K A Nitz
WHANGANUI, NEW ZEALAND

Immanuel Kants Vorlesungen über Psychologie
published with an introduction by Carl du Prel:
"Kants mystische Weltanschauung"
in German 1889

ISBN: 978-0-473-71485-7

https://kanitzpublishing.com

Table of Contents

Translator's Note

All translations in the following are my own unless otherwise noted. All references to Kant and Swedenborg in the introduction have been adapted to refer to German editions which are easily found online.

As present-day readers often lack the background in the classical languages which Kant's students would have had, the first appearances of Latin terms have been accompanied by rough translations in square brackets, and a similar approach has been taken to the titles of lesser-known German books referred to in the text.

I have translated the word *Sinnlichkeit*, which is usually translated as sensuality or sensuousness, but in the context here is related more to a sensory-ness than a sensual-ness, as sensoriality.

Foreword

In the year 1821 a book appeared under the title *Immanuel Kants Vorlesungen über Metaphysik* [Kant's Lectures on Metaphysics] (1821, Erfurt: Keyser), its printing supported by the publisher of Kant's *Vorlesungen über Philosophische Religionslehre* [Lectures on Philosophical Religious Doctrine].

It was K. H. Ludwig Poelitz, teacher of constitutional law and founder of the Leipzig city library who published the book.

In itself a new printing of the entire book would not need a special reason. Rather I may justify myself that I only publish anew here a section — admittedly the longest and most original — on psychology. It happens because Kant in the other sections (ontology, cosmology, rational theology) in comparison to his writings in the complete editions does not present anything essentially new, just that here is speech reads more definitely and, as comes with academic lectures, is less provided with critical reflections. The lectures on psychology by contrast — which take up pages 125 to 261 in Poelitz's edition — offer the possessors of the complete edition of Kant not only something essentially new, but even something so odd that I already considered it necessary for this reason to provide this new printing with a longer, more explanatory introduction. The content of this introduction will also inform the reader over why I consider directly myself appointed for this publication. The reason is that any other editor, as valuable as I may also think their work is, would certainly have disregarded precisely those points of view dealt with by me. I can claim that above all because I at the moment I am still treading my philosophical path quite alone.

The circumstance that Kant's lectures could end up forgotten alone proves already that no great value has been attached to them. In part that can even be comprehended and excused, because the "Lectures on Psychology" are only now receiving real interest, almost seventy years after their publication by Poelitz, indeed they can only now be understood, and thus be appropriately valued. Instead of thus justifying this new printing only in general on account that everything which comes from Kant deserves our interest, I can justify this publication on quite special grounds:

1. First of all, the book by Poelitz can directly be considered to have disappeared. The first to have discovered it again and mention it several times was Dr Hans Vaihinger, at the time Professor of Philosophy in Halle*. Later Professor Erdmann directed attention to it†; he discussed it, however, only from the standpoint of Kant philology. Also Ueberweg‡ mentions the book. Nonetheless the knowledge of it remained limited to a few Kant specialists; the greater philosophical public knew nothing of it. Within my circle of acquaintances the book has even escaped professors of the subject. I did not find it in the Munich city library, even in the library in Dresden it is missing, and I could only obtain it from antiquarian booksellers after a long search. In short, the book by Poelitz is as good as unknown.

2. Kant's "lectures" decide conclusively the dispute over how Kant thought about Swedenborg. In his other writings Kant twice expressed his view over this remarkable scholar and seer, but not entirely consistently — in the "Träume eines Geistersehers" [Dreams of a Visionary] and in the letter to Miss von Knobloch; in the one he judged him less favourably, in the other more favourably. Now the librarian Tafel in Tübingen wanted to demonstrate that the latter letter was written later than the "Dreams", that accordingly the more

---

*   Hans Vaihinger, ed., *Kommentar zu Kants Kritik der reinen Vernunft zum hundertjährigen Jubiläum derselben* (Stuttgart: W. Spemann, 1881), I:22.

†   Benno Erdmann, "Eine unbeachtet gebliebene Quelle zur Entwicklungsgeschichte Kants," *Philosophische Monatshefte* 19 (1883): 129–44; furthermore: Benno Erdmann, "Mitteilungen über Kants metaphysischen Standpunkt in der Zeit um 1774," *Philosophische Monatshefte* 20 (1884): 65–97.

‡   Friedrich Ueberweg, *Grundriss der Geschichte der Philosophie: von Thales bis auf die Gegenwart*, 7th ed. (Leipzig: E.S. Mittler & Sohn, 1886), 3:228.

unfavourable judgement was lifted by the later, more favourable one. Against that, the matter would stand completely reversed if — as others claim — the letter had an earlier date.

The mere existence of this dispute now proves that everyone who has participated in it did not know of Poelitz's book; Kant's "lectures" in fact fall, and indeed indisputably, in a later period than both the "Dreams" and that letter. Thus anyone who knows Poelitz's book need not get mixed up in that dispute at all; for in the lectures on psychology Kant delivers a third and final judgement over Swedenborg, and indeed the most favourable of the three. He relinquishes in it the visions of Swedenborg, but adopts fully his metaphysical explanation of humanity.

3. Through Kant's lectures on psychology his text "Träume eines Geistersehers" [Dreams of a Visionary] is put in a new light. You would indeed think that this text was written so clearly that a false interpretation would be obviated anyway; but the aversion of our century towards mystical thoughts has brought about a misunderstanding of the "Dreams" nonetheless. They have been represented as a high-spirited play of his mind with superstition, the accent has been placed on Kant's negations and the clear positions have been neglected. The "lectures" show now, however, that these positions were meant very seriously; for the positive components of the "Dreams" agree exactly with their detailed depiction in the lectures on psychology, and the wavering of Kant in the former is brought to a standstill in the latter.

The Enlightenment did everything to bring the personality of Swedenborg into discredit and thus make out the slant of the "Dreams" as if Kant were the gravedigger of any belief in spirits. On the other hand, today the mystics appeal to the "Dreams" for their own advantage. The question of which side the greater right of appeal lies on is decided by Kant's lectures on psychology in favour of the mystics, since they deliver the indisputable proof that the Enlightenment misunderstood Kant's "Träume eines Geistersehers" [Dreams of a Visionary]. Kant is rejecting, or at least sceptical with respect to the protruding of the spirit world into our own which the current spiritism teaches; to the contrary, for Kant the protruding of the human into the spirit world was not subject to the smallest doubt, rather it results from his definition of the human, and his views on it agree precisely with those of Swedenborg. The facts of somnambulism discovered since then, however, have confirmed the correctness of these views empirically.

4. Some apparent inconsistency of Kant, which was discovered by his interpreters and censured, is now put in a different light by the lectures on psychology.

It has already been frequently remarked that Kant did not always hold precisely to the critical median between dogmatism and scepticism which he allocated to philosophy, so that in fact opposed parties could call on him. It was assumed to be understandable in itself that all the dogmatic elements of his philosophy point back to the *past*, in that the hatched chicken of the critical system still bore fragments of the dogmatic eggshell on its wings. But already the circumstance that such wavering by Kant was also found in his critical and post-critical periods betrays a second source of it, concerning which the hostile rebuke of an inconsistency of Kant's does not apply. Kant's lectures on psychology, in which his dogmatic language is heard very definitely, are eminently suited to accounting for this second source, so that in fact the appearance can arise of Kant thereby falling back on a long since surmounted standpoint.

Under these circumstances the question first obtains interest of from which year these lectures originate, whether from the pre-critical or post-critical periods. Because the reactionary appearance adheres to them quite considerably, Professor Erdmann sought to prove that the drawing up of these lectures fell approximately in the year 1774, thus in the pre-critical period. But assuming even that it were so, the lectures though were *held* in the post-critical period. The editor Poelitz used for them two sets of notes from the years 1788 and 1789, and a third set of notes — which is presently found in the possession of the Pastor Albrecht Krause — likewise originates from the year 1788. A longer fragment from them, whose transcription I owe to the kindness of Professor W. Sellin in Hamburg, shows almost word-for-word identity with the text by Poelitz[*]. Accordingly the appearance arose of Kant having directly within the post-critical period — namely seven years after the *Critique of Pure Reason* and two years before the *Critique of Judgement* — again carried out a complete reactionary turn which was seen as a regrettable inconsistency, and this was without doubt also the reason why these lectures were allowed to fall into such complete oblivion. They are in fact to a high degree dogmatic. Anyone thus who, as I, did not believe Kant capable of logical inconsistency is compelled to let the dogmatism of this "psychology" flow from another source. Instead of explaining it as the relapse to a surmounted standpoint, we must see in it anticipations of ideas which yet lay in the future, and to which at Kant's time the empirical confirmation could not be given.

This talent of anticipating ideas which indeed could only be established dogmatically in his time, but which were later confirmed by experience, was something Kant possessed to an eminent degree. As an astronomer he theorised the nebula origins of the universe which were only discovered later, as physicist the law of conservation of force, as biologist the organic theory of evolution. Should Kant now not have possessed at all this capacity for anticipation, which he showed so many times in the natural sciences, precisely in his own actual subject, as a philosopher? That can certainly not be assumed, and I will show in the introduction that he possessed it precisely most of all where the appearance of a dogmatic relapse is the greatest.

This mixing up of a prophetic sight with a relapse could only happen to the interpreters of Kant because they do not know that area of facts which Kant prophetically indicated and in which the empirical confirmation of his anticipations lies. The book of Poelitz has on the other hand remained unknown to the mystics for their part too — Fichte, Ulrici, Hoff-

---

[*] An original manuscript by Kant probably never existed. For the planning of his lectures he used textbooks, or he also only brought along a small sheet of paper on which his train of thought was laid down in an abridged fashion. (Reinhold Bernhard Jachmann, *Immanuel Kant geschildert in Briefen an einen Freund* (Königsberg: F. Nicolovius, 1804), 27; Ludwig Ernst Borowski, *Darstellung des Lebens und Charakters Immanuel Kant's* (Königsberg: F. Nicolovius, 1804), 33.) Through the new [German] spelling implemented in the present edition, the reverence towards Kant is thus not injured.

mann, Perty, Zöllner, and Hellenbach would have had the greatest interest in referring to the lectures on psychology, and would have certainly done so if they had known of Poelitz's book — and thus show then again that it would become philosophy just as well to study mysticism as mysticism philosophy in return.

5. But this is now the point which I must emphasise above all: Kant anticipated in his lectures on psychology the modern mystical philosophy. For that reason his lectures are precisely of current interest for our times, indeed their actual sense can only be understood today.

Modern mysticism encompasses the areas of animal magnetism, hypnotism, somnambulism, and spiritualism. The scientific research into these areas fell in our century, thus they remained foreign to Kant. They are likewise foreign, even though for other reasons, to our current academic faculties, although they should all have the greatest interest in them; for this modern mysticism, amenable to experiment, does not bring new ideas perhaps only to philosophy and psychology, but rather also to cultural history, medicine, jurisprudence, indeed to physics, chemistry, botany, etc. A philosophical examination of mysticism now results, however, in a series of positions with respect to the metaphysical nature of humanity, and the most important of these positions are found almost completely in Kant's lectures on psychology.

Thus Kant showed himself to be a prophet directly where his interpreters suspected the opposite, namely relapse into the old dogmatism which they thought permitted to rebuke so much that they — in order to protect Kant! — allowed his lectures to fall into oblivion. Even the few Kant specialists to whom Poelitz's book was well-known did not acknowledge the agreement of the Kantian mysticism with the modern one, because they just did not know the latter, indeed had contempt for it. Anyone, for example, who reads the mentioned treatises of Professor Erdmann, but then reads the introduction to the present book, could only perhaps be reminded by the name Poelitz that we are both discussing one and the same book. Erdmann can just only see a regrettable relapse in Kant's lectures on psychology and leaves the mysticism of them undiscussed; but I place the accent just on this mysticism because Kant here proves himself to be a mighty prophet. *Duo, si legunt idem, non est idem.* [Whenever two read the same thing, it is not the same.]

Kant in fact drew up in his lectures on psychology an entire system of mysticism which, however, was only left as a skeleton because the confirming facts were missing for him. It received no attention because one saw in it only a collection of dogmatic ideas, of which there is indeed no lack in philosophy. The neglect of the mystical studies has thus led our philosophy to a false interpretation of Kant. When Poelitz published these lectures this conception was at least excusable. But today it is not so anymore, the prophetic vision of Kant which lies in them must immediately become clear to anyone who is well-versed in mysticism; for the agreement of the lectures on psychology with that system which has been built inductively on the facts of somnambulism is in fact in all essential points a complete one.

Certainly Kant deviates in it from his critical standpoint, which only permitted him such metaphysical ideas as are to be derived from facts of experience. But that Kant expected such facts from the future, indeed considered them in his time to be possible, follows already from his occupation with Swedenborg and, as we will see, he gave expression to this expectation in the "Dreams". Under this viewpoint, however, Kant's inconsistency appears not as regrettable weakness, but rather deserves our admiration.

The demand that Kant should have completely muzzled himself through his critical system is entirely unpsychological. For admittedly he wanted to make an end to the uncertain fumbling around in philosophy and hence wrote his critique which amounted to a provisional sacrifice of metaphysical insights with the inclusion of further experience; but with that a philosopher ends up at base in a psychological contradiction with himself. What makes him a philosopher namely is just the capacity for wonder and the metaphysical need arising from that. The result of this need should now, however, be the acknowledgement that it is not to be satisfied. Such a complete sacrifice cannot be expected of a philosopher; he would thereby give up his own nature, as it were

have to travel out of his intellectual skin. He will thus eat of
the forbidden fruit, and indeed sacrifice metaphysical certainties, but not probabilities and possibilities. He will draw up
hypotheses, and leave it to the future to deliver their proof
through the expansion of experience. Hence we find strewn in
various writings of Kant metaphysical speculations; but they
are only the seeds which were not developed. In the lectures
on psychology, however, he joined up these seeds into an organic whole.

It will thus turn out for the reader well-versed in mysticism as it did for me — I was completely stunned when I saw
Kant speculating in a way as if the facts of modern mysticism
were well-known to him, and found in his lectures on psychology the most essential points which are found in my own
writings as the consequences from the factual material of
mysticism. I certainly had easy and only inductive work;
Kant, however, could only immerse himself intuitively in the
puzzle of humanity, and nevertheless struck the right thing.

I do not expect nonetheless that now modern mysticism
will achieve quicker acceptance because of its now provable
agreement with Kantian ideas; indeed it has no right at all to
desire its acceptance on that basis, it must rather prove its
own worth by virtue of its agreement with experience. But I
will nevertheless draw an advantage as an isolated philosophical representative of mysticism from Kant: the blows namely
which fell on mysticism — there are very many such among
them for which the students have a particular expression —
fell not only on me, but also on Kant. That will bring some of
my opponents to their senses; they will at least not be permitted to assume anymore that anyone who entertains mystical
ideas must have directly lost their mind. The modesty which
they should have drawn already from their ignorance in these
things, which they have not given to me though, they will perhaps now give to a Kant. Under these circumstances my opponents will at least change their manner of attack — they
will deny me the priority of my ideas. But I will not experience that as a rebuke; I am myself and indeed the first who
brought this priority of Kant to light as soon as I discovered it
myself.

But if I admired the philosopher of Königsberg previously already for having preserved in his philosophy all existing systems *in nuce* [in a nutshell], I admire him now all the more since I see that a circle of thought excited first by the facts of experience of modern mysticism was foreseen by him in its essential features.

Silz in Tyrol in August 1888.

Carl du Prel.

Introduction: Kant's Mystical World View

Weak parties seek to strengthen their standing by citing in their favour remarks of famous men or even holding up the entire personalities of them as forerunners and claiming them for themselves.

I am then also prepared to hear the following examination of Kant's mystical world view declared to have come from the feelings of weakness of my own mysticism. But readers who undertake their reading without a priori malice will then soon acknowledge that my attempt is to be taken somewhat more seriously; for I will not read a new mystical sense into the well-known writings of Kant, but rather only place the undoubtedly mystical ideas of Kant, which are found strewn in his writings, into context here, but then obtain the proof from the lectures of Kant on psychology, which had fallen into oblivion, that Kant himself gave in them — in so far as this was possible in his time — mysticism the form of a self-contained system. I will call on the writings of Kant from every period of his development, from the pre-critical, critical, and post-critical periods — on the "Gedanken von der wahren Schätzung der lebendigen Kräfte" [Thoughts on the True Estimation of Living Forces], on the "Träume eines Geistersehers" [Dreams of a Visionary], on the "Kritik der reinen Vernunft" [Critique of Pure Reason], on the "Kritik der praktischen Vernunft" [Critique of Practical Reason], but especially on the "Vorlesungen über Psychologie" [Lectures on Psychology]. With that it will then be shown that Kant tended throughout his entire life towards mystical views, whereby admittedly the lack of empirical factual material was a great hindrance to him, but which he finally rounded off in his psychology into a metaphysics of humanity; for Kant did not treat psychology in the vulgar sense, but rather for him it was about transcendental psychology. In this, however, Kant appears admittedly to be a quite original forerunner of the current mysticism, and indeed to a degree which I myself would not at all have guessed at until recently.

Certainly Kant's actual life's work was the critical work; he examined the extent, boundaries, and abilities of human reason, directed this reason towards experience, and forbade it from taking speculative pleasure trips. But such a powerful intellect as Kant cannot ever condemn itself to metaphysical lack of opinion; the view is above all out of the question that that drive which is the psychological basis of all philosophy — the metaphysical need — shall have been directly lacking in the greatest of philosophers. If moreover the critical Kant taught that before we pass to the object of cognition, first the organ of cognition must be examined, that we must thus examine the human before we explain the world, then the mystical Kant also retained the same direction and recognised "know yourself!" as the real entrance to metaphysics. It was for him as a mystic firstly to do with the puzzle of humanity; in this area, however, he had himself barred from speculations, at least in the form of hypotheses, all the less so than indeed with the most complicated and puzzling form of nature, the human, whom the wisdom of the ancients recognised as microcosm, the greatest hope also existed of arriving by further penetration at new factual material by which such metaphysical hypotheses could yet receive their empirical confirmation. This hope of Kant was outstandingly justified in fact, and the reader to whom the lectures on psychology are offered here in a new edition can convince himself that Kant hit it on the head with his metaphysical hypotheses; for his intuitive solution of the puzzle of humanity agrees with the inductive one of the current mysticism.

The idea of Kant that the perceivable world is only the appearance of a "thing in itself" unknown to us, that space and time are only forms of our cognition, is mystic in the eminent sense, and to that extent you can admittedly call Kant a mystic. But I will in no way make my task so simple. With the unrecognisability of the "thing in itself", the transcendental idealism of Kant is indeed a mysticism, but yet without positive content. But I, as the at present still very isolated representative of the mystical philosophy, can only be helped by the positive views of Kant and their agreement with my own mysticism.

Such an agreement would be all the more valuable when the entire arsenal of facts of hypnotism, somnambulism, and spiritualism stood at my disposal, from which my mystical views succeed in being derived inductively with a little acumen and logic, whereas Kant merely by virtue of the profundity peculiar to him obtained just such views over the nature of humanity from which in reverse the mystical facts can be derived deductively.

The opponents will certainly say that philosophical intuitions, even if they are so profound, can claim no scientific worth as long as they do not receive the sanction of the natural sciences. But even if it is correct that ideas are only then our own property when they are proven to be necessary connections of the system, that institutions only receive their actual worth when they are also founded on the path of logic and are confirmed by experience, then even our modern science should have treated these Kantian intuitions according to Goethe's words:

> What you have inherited from your fathers,
> Acquire it in order to possess it.

It just depends on who has intuitions, and that such a Kant must not be underestimated is shown in that Kant, as Zöllner has proven, anticipated a series of the most important natural science achievements of our century, even intuitively recognising the fundamental principles of our natural sciences — the preservation of force and the theory of evolution. His philosophical intuitions, however, have proven just as valuable; for all post-Kantian systems have grown from the "Critique of Pure Reason" — Fichte, Schelling, Hegel, Herbart, and Schopenhauer took Kant as their starting point; Hartmann, Hellenbach, and Bahnsen branch off in turn from Schopenhauer. The entire thought of our century, philosophical and scientific, is found thus *in nuce* with Kant. In his philosophy is found in intuitive form the buds which since then have developed into blossoms. Brilliant ideas are always fertile in that they, placed in a foreign brain, as it were bring about an intellectual parthenogenesis, and it simply lies in the historical position of such a philosopher that with him such ideas can only appear in intuitive form. This is itself the mark of genius, anticipating truths and drawing wide-reaching inferences from meagre factual material, whereas the mere talent needs entire wagon loads of facts to draw small inferences, and first finds the truth when science has already brought all the data necessary for it.

That now, however, such various systems have grown from Kant is not perhaps to be explained thus that Kant abandoned himself in an unprincipled way to his ideas when he drew up metaphysical speculations, but rather the seeds lay enclosed in him, like in a biological archetype which differentiates itself into various types; and if I now also demonstrate the seeds of the mystical world view in Kant, in that lies only the acknowledgement of his genius, not perhaps a need for love and affection in the feeling of my weakness. The mystical world view has to prove its legitimacy from itself, and for that the proof of a mystical seed of thought with such a famous forerunner in no way suffices. Meanwhile I attach only modest hopes to this proof — today namely even scholars still see in mysticism only the spawn of perverse thinking, and these people could at least be brought somewhat to their senses if they see that all the main points of the mystical world view agree with views which are found strewn in the works of Kant, whom to accuse of perverse thinking would be daring though. But they will not even be able to say that I misunderstand Kant, for I will cite his own words.

They will indeed as before deny the facts of mysticism, which is all the easier if you deliberately go out of their way; they will also reproach my philosophical valuation of these facts, but since the agreement with Kant is not to be denied, the unprejudiced reader will acknowledge though that Kant would only have needed the material of the facts of experience in order to make from his mystical intuitions, which he preserved his whole life long, the crux of a metaphysical system which would have coincided completely with that of the present mysticism.

If they thus might deny me originality and reproach me for holding on to Kant's coat-tails, I will though be content if they only confess that these coat-tails in fact exist, and that I will admittedly prove, and it comes down to that alone. —

The dogma and the premise of materialism is that there is nothing supernatural in the entire world, but rather only matter; everything which occurs in experience can accordingly only be modifications of matter — the human spirit, for example, is only a modification of the brain. This view leaves no room for mysticism. — The premise of mysticism on the other hand is that the sensory and reality — considered identical by the materialists — do not coincide, that there is next to the world perceivable by the senses, yet another; next to the ways of sensory cognition, yet another; next to the powers and laws of the sensory world, yet other powers and laws.

Now how does Kant stand in relation to this alternative?

Anyone who at least assumes the possibility that reality rises up above the sensory has no occasion to write a "Critique of Pure Reason". Anyone who is of the view that the real world and our world of imagination coincide qualitatively and quantitatively has no need to counter the dogmatic philosophy with a critical one; he can confidently go immediately up to the objects of cognition and philosophise about the world and need not first examine the organ of cognition for its capabilities. In this respect the "Critique of Pure Reason" already has the mystical idea as its logical assumption. Since, however, Kant remained unfamiliar with the facts of mysticism — mesmerism only fell partly into his time — we will have to expect from him for the moment as mystical concession only that he confesses the logical possibility of another world.

We find this idea clearly expressed by Kant. In his text "Gedanken von der wahren Schätzung der lebendigen Kräfte" [Thoughts on the True Estimation of Living Forces], §8 has the heading [which translates to]:

"It is in a properly metaphysical sense true that more than one world can exist." He works this out in more detail: "Because you cannot say that something is a part of a whole when it has no connection at all with the remaining parts (for otherwise no difference would exist between a real union and an imagined one), but the world is an actually assembled nature, thus a substance which is not bound to any other thing in the entire world will also not belong to the world at all, it is then in thought, i.e. it will not be a part of the same thing. If many are of the same nature, standing in no connection to any thing in the world, having a relationship only against one another, then from it arises a quite peculiar whole, they make up a quite peculiar world. It was thus not correctly spoken when one in the auditoriums of wisdom always taught that no more than a single world could exist in the metaphysical sense. It is really possible that God created many worlds, even taken in the properly metaphysical meaning. Hence it remains undecided whether such even really exist or not."

Further on, Kant explains that no space, no expansion would exist if the substances did not have powers to work outside themselves; that without powers no connection, without this no order, without this no space would exist; that furthermore the threefold dimensioning of space turns up because the forces of the earthly substances decrease with the square of the distance. From a different law of force a different dimension of space would also follow, thus a world for itself. But since now even our soul belongs to those substances which receive their impressions according to the law of the square of distance, it thus follows from it that we are incapable of imagining a space of more than three dimensions. According to Kant it is improbable that there is only the three dimensional world; there could be as many of them as types of space are possible whose inhabitants distinguish themselves by the type of cognition the way the inhabitants of our world do so through the degrees of cognition. Finally Kant in-

---

*   Immanuel Kant, *Immanuel Kant's sämmtliche Werke*, ed. Karl Rosenkrantz and Friedrich Wilhelm Schubert (Leipzig: L. Voss, 1838), 5:24-26.

dicated already at the conclusion of the "Allgemeine Naturge-schichte und Theorie des Himmels" [Universal Natural History and Theory of the Heavens] the possibility of an absolutely non-spatial world. This spirit world would be closed to a cognition subject to the conditions of a spatial world. Only in a single case could an insight into this spirit world take place, namely when the soul possesses, other than the type of cognition which befits the spatial world, the type of cognition of non-spatial intelligences, i.e. thus when the soul would number itself among the inhabitants of that spirit world. In this case immortality would be taken in the sense of a heightening of human nature, not perhaps only as moving from planet to planet within our world.

The question about the where of this non-physical world did not exist for Kant because it was just part of its nature to not need a space. The characteristic of impenetrability only applies to the physical; thus the spirit world could very well be within the same space as the physical world. That is part of the concept of the non-physical. But the same applies also to the inhabitants of this spirit world who thus could be en-closed in a material organism.

Just as we have as humans the physical senses, the inhab-itants of the spirit world would have the non-physical senses corresponding to these, which would not be bound to any matter or space. The physical senses could not have any knowledge of the non-physical world, and only the mere concept of a non-physical cognition is permitted to us. For the actuality of such a one, however, in the case where our soul would belong to the spirit world, that extraordinary way of experience would be necessary which the visionaries pretend to possess. Kant did not deny the possibility of such a non-physical type of cognition, as it were a second sight of our soul. He wrote to Miss von Knobloch: "As much is certain that, notwithstanding all the stories of phenomena and the actions of the spirit world, of which a great quantity of the most probable are known to me, I have considered though each time the rule of sound reason to be most appropriate for steering to the negative; not as if I intended to have realised the impossibility of them (for how little is known to us yet of

the nature of a spirit?), but rather because they are not altogether sufficiently proven."

Even in the "Träume eines Geistersehers" [Dreams of a
Visionary], the concept of the pneumatic in contrast to the
physical lies for Kant in that a pneumatic substance, without
supplanting a physical substance, could though be in the
same space. If thus a pneumatic world were to exist, it would
not actually be a spatial other side, no lack of space would
thus exist for it, no less than a housing shortage would exist
for us if we humans were likewise pneumatic substances.

Kant called pneumatic substances immaterial and, when
they had reason, spirits. It was now not at all unthinkable to
him that such spirits could enter into physical beings since
they indeed act in space, but are in themselves non-spatial.
Kant considered not only humans, but all living beings to be
such beings, physical and at the same time non-physical. This
idea, that the human is both physical and pneumatic, Kant
called "charming", and he said that he "cannot give [it] up,
nor wants to" on aesthetic and moral grounds. Such beings
thus lead a double life, but in such a way that the two ways of
being remain mutually foreign to each other. At least the
pneumatic way of being must remain foreign to the physical
human; the gift of being conscious within the earthly existence at the same time of one's pneumatic nature could in any
case only be extremely rare, could only occur as an extraordinary exception.

From these remarks by Kant, it is now clearly recognised
that he did *not* base his proof of the soul and the spirituality
of the soul on the normal sensory manner of cognition, so
that I can thus call on Kant for my opinion that only a transcendental psychology can deliver a proof of the soul.

I have only pulled together in brief these views of Kant
which are found strewn in the cited texts* because my opponents will not accept my referring to the pre-critical Kant anyway. But before I let the critical and post-critical Kant speak, I
must go into the "Träume eines Geistersehers" [Dreams of a
Visionary].

---

*   Cf. Robert Zimmermann, *Kant und der Spiritismus* (Vienna: Karl Gerold's Son,
1879).

xx

Up to now we have seen that Kant did not deny *a priori* any possibility that humans become during their lifetime conscious at the same time of their pneumatic nature and thereby come into contact with the spiritual realm — said in a modern way: that a transcendental idea, overstepping the threshold of perception, becomes a mental idea — and if there is such a being, then its spiritual perceptions, in order to become conscious of them as a human, must clothe themselves in the sensory forms, without therefore becoming mere hallucinations. Kant even surveyed the relevant literature so that "a great quantity of the most probable stories [were] familiar" to him; but the empirical evidence appeared inadequate to him.

Kant had come so far with his independent ideas, when the visionary Swedenborg made a name for himself, whereby his thoughts were steered again to this matter. The abilities ascribed to Swedenborg corresponded entirely to the concept defined by Kant of a being which belonged simultaneously to two worlds. He wrote to Swedenborg, and since he received no answer, he asked an English friend he had gotten to know in Königsberg to seek out the visionary and report to him about him, and he then also wrote several letters to Kant about it. It suffices to cite from these reports a case of Swedenborg's visionary gift. Kant wrote to Miss von Knobloch:

"The following incident, however, seems to me to have by all means the greatest validity and really removes any prevarication from every conceivable doubt. It was in the year 1756 when Mr von Swedenborg, arriving from England towards the end of the month of September on a Saturday at 4 o'clock in the afternoon, disembarked in Gothenburg. Mr William Castel invited him to his place and also a company of fifteen persons. Mr von Swedenborg had gone out at 6 o'clock in the evening and returned to the room discoloured and shaken. He said there had just then been a disastrous fire in Stockholm on the island of Södermalm (Gothenburg lies about 50 miles from Stockholm) and the fire was spreading. He was restless and went out often. He said that the house of one of his friends, whom he named, already lay in ashes and his own house was in danger. At 8 o'clock, after he had gone out again, he said joyfully, 'thank God, the fire has been extinguished, three doors from my house!' — This news strongly moved the entire city and especially the company and they informed the Governor of it that same evening. On the morning of the Sunday Swedenborg was called to the Governor. The latter questioned him about the matter. Swedenborg described the fire exactly, how it began, how it had stopped, and the period of its lasting. The same day the news ran through the entire city where, because the Governor paid attention to it, it caused a still greater stir, since many were concerned on account of their friends or on account of their property. On the Monday evening a dispatch rider arrived who had been sent to Gothenburg by the merchants in Stockholm during the fire. In the letters the fire had been described entirely in the said way. On Tuesday morning a royal courier came to the Governor with the report of the fire, of the losses which it caused, and the houses which it affected; no different from the report which Swedenborg had given at the same time, for the fire had been extinguished at 8 o'clock.

What can you adduce against the credibility of this incident? The friend who writes of this to me has investigated all of it not only in Stockholm, but himself about two months ago in Gothenburg where he knows the best houses very well and where he could inform himself completely from an entire city in which in the short time from 1756 most of the eyewitnesses still live."[*]

As advantageous as this conduct of Kant contrasts with that of our enlightened professors who, if they even consider it worth their effort to talk of mystical phenomena, do not even shy from moral attacks so as to be rid of such reports. Before me lies the text of such a professor in which it can be read word-for-word: "Anyone who knows people knows that Swedenborg *had either himself lit the fire* recognised by him

---

[*]   Immanuel Kant, "Träume eines Geistersehers, erläutert durch Träume der Metaphysik," in *Imanuel Kant's vermischte Schriften*, vol. 2 (Halle: Regersche Buchhandlung, 1799), 315–16.

in Stockholm, in order to give himself the reputation of a supernaturally gifted human, *or that he came across the knowledge by accident.*"[*] Now since, however, from the report of Kant it follows that there can be no talk at all of an accident in that indeed the distant view of Swedenborg, just landed in Gothenburg, agreed in all given details with the reality, Professor Hoppe must in a logical way assume that Swedenborg had the fire lit. You can only respond to that that if Kant himself were to stand before the alternative of considering himself to be naive or calling Swedenborg — whose character itself stood in the greatest esteem with his opponents — without any proof a rogue, he would with his strict love of justice have cheerfully grasped for the first hypothesis as the simpler one. The procedure of calling Swedenborg a fool is also much beloved in order to be rid of this uncomfortable man. This is done, for example, by Professor Zimmermann; indeed he even holds this opinion as being from Kant himself, in that he says, "It is certainly no accident that Kant right at the time when he must have been reading Swedenborg's writings [...] wrote his 'Versuch über die Krankheiten des Kopfes' [Essay over the Ailments of the Head]. The explanation which Kant gives of the insane, especially of fantasists, fits exactly for Swedenborg."[†] This claim by Zimmermann now has, however, not even the value of a mere hypothesis; for it is directly provable that Kant was brought to his treatment of the ailments of the head by a half-mad enthusiast who, wandering about with a herd of goats, came to Königsberg and gave voice to quotes from the Bible, especially of the prophets, for which reason the people gave him the name of the goat-prophet.[‡]

Kant thus devoted his attention to the case of Swedenborg because he hoped to find the sought-after empirical confirmation of his views over the nature of humanity which we have already gotten to know. For even if at the time the "Critique of Pure Reason", which expressed the relinquishment by philo-

---

[*]   Johann Ignaz Hoppe, *Einige Aufklärungen über das Hellsehen des Unbewussten im menschlichen Denken: mit besondrer Beziehung auf das "schottische Gesicht"; auf Grund von Untersuchungen* (Freiburg im Breisgau: Herder, 1872), 14.

[†]   Zimmermann, *Kant und der Spiritismus*, 62.

[‡]   Borowski, *Darstellung des Lebens und Charakters Immanuel Kant's*, 64, 206–10.

sophy of metaphysical insights, was already maturing in his intellect, such a relinquishment only refers to the metaphysical certainties and also applies only subject to future experience. By comparison, Kant himself still remained entirely free after his major work to engage himself in the area of metaphysical possibilities and probabilities; already from psychological grounds, indeed from the concept of the philosopher who cannot be thought of without the deep urge for metaphysical insights, it follows that Kant had already prepared a metaphysics at least for his private use. Some of that we have already become acquainted with; he confirms it, however, expressly in the "Träume eines Geistersehers" [Dreams of a Visionary], though still more clearly in his lectures.

Unfortunately, however, the ideas of our philosophers are not well-known to the public, but rather mostly known only through second-hand descriptions. Anyone namely who suffers in the area of philosophy for a lack of their own ideas busies themselves mostly with analysing and describing the ideas of their predecessors. Every newly minted academic believes himself firstly to be supposed to gratify the readers with a history of philosophy or at least of a period of it, and unfortunately more such books are also read than the philosophers themselves because, as Börne already said, the Germans would rather read a book over a book than the book itself. But anyone now who wants to convince themselves over what distortions the original ideas of our philosophers have often suffered by their passing through an alien mind, they can do nothing better than to read Kant's "Träume eines Geistersehers" [Dreams of a Visionary], but then to read what the presentations from second-hand make of it. The ideas of Kant are barely to be recognised anymore; they look in these reproductions like a picture by Raphael seen through distorting glass. The reader learns there that Kant in the "Dreams" made a blow against superstition from which the latter will not recover, and Professor Rosenkrantz says: "When you read Kant's such well-written and well-grounded treatise, you might, on account of the excitement which has in our time made similar distorted pictures of the absolute truth, wish for the simple and inexpensive reprinting of such classic texts as antidote [...] for such things should finally also be able to be written once and for all time."[*]

You just find in any book only oneself; you keep from it only what you are comprehend and more or less already vaguely knew; the rest you let fall. Since now the science of our century is so averse to the belief in spirits, they thus also accentuate in Kant's "Dreams" only that which confirms this tendency, and overlook the other half. The wish of Professor Rosenkrantz is now fulfilled; the "Dreams"have been taken up in Reclams Universalbibliothek and are to be obtained for about 20 pfennigs[†]. But now should what Kant says there be written down once and for all time, that must apply to the entire treatise, not merely those sentences which fit with the prejudices of our century. The readers can now easily convince themselves, however, that Kant does not merely appear in the "Dreams" as a crusher, does not set out mere negations, but rather very clear and definite positions, namely such mystical ideas which indeed only have the value of intuitions, thus no absolute power of proof, but of which Kant just could not free himself.

Certainly Kant himself cites the words of Aristotle: "When we wake, we have a common world; but when we dream, each has his own" — and adds: "I think you should probably be able to turn the last sentence around and say: if of various people each has his own world, then it is to be presumed that they are dreaming."[‡] Since now the world in the head of any one metaphysician represents itself differently, you can say of them that they are dreaming, and because now Kant must confess that likewise of his own metaphysics which agrees with the theories of Swedenborg, he gave, speaking of both, his text the title: "Träume eines Geistersehers, erläutert durch Träume der Metaphysik" [Dreams of a Visionary, Elucidated through the Dreams of Metaphysics]. Kant thus ascribed to his own metaphysical ideas no greater value than to the metaphysical ideas of a visionary like Swedenborg which were just

---

*   Kant, *Immanuel Kant's sämmtliche Werke*, 7:147.

†   [Tr.: the equivalent of being published as a Penguin paperback during the late 20th century.]

‡   Kant, "Träume eines Geistersehers, erläutert durch Träume der Metaphysik," 292.

XXV

as difficult to prove. But he did not deny — and it is about this here — that he entertained such dreams, and he confessed that his metaphysics had a quite striking similarity to the theory of Swedenborg.

Swedenborg claimed to have had contact with spirits, and Kant, long before he had heard of Swedenborg, had occupied himself with the question of under which conditions it would be absolutely possible that a human could have insights into the intelligible* world. He came to the conclusion that it was only possible under a single condition, namely if the human were simultaneously a physical being and a member of the spiritual realm. Just this now, however, was Kant's opinion not merely in reference to humanity, but to all living creatures. Hence he said:

> "I confess that I am very much inclined to claim the existence of immaterial natures in the world and to place my soul itself in the class of these beings [...] Now since these immaterial beings are self-acting principles, therefore substances and natures existing for themselves, that consequence to which you next arrive is this: that they might make up amongst each other directly united perhaps a large whole which you can call the immaterial world (*mundus intelligibilis*) [...] This immaterial world can thus be seen as a whole existing for itself, whose parts stand among one another in mutual combination and community, also without the mediation of physical things, so that this last relationship is contingent and only entitled to a few, indeed, where they are also found, not hindered, that not just the immaterial beings, which act in one another through the mediation of matter, stand apart from this in a special and universal connection and exercise every time a mutual influence amongst each other as immaterial beings so that their relationship by means of matter is only contingent and rests on a special divine institution, that is on the other hand natural and indissoluble."†

---

*   [Tr.: intelligible, in a philosophical sense, means it can only be understood by the intellect and not by the senses.]

Kant could thus occupy himself with this problem without receiving the reproach of falling back into the dogmatism which had been put aside by him. For even if the human knows nothing of his pneumatic nature, because the intelligible consciousness is not encompassed by the sensory, this unconsciousness could though possibly suffer an exception, because indeed the sensory human and the intelligible subject are at base just one and the same being. For the possibility of a dual consciousness in one and the same being, Kant could call on the sleepwalkers.* Had he known of the artificial somnambulism, then he would have used this for comparison with its dual consciousness and memoryless awakening and would have said that we likewise forget with the incarnation of our intelligible existence the way the somnambulist awakes without memory from the ecstasy. By comparison, Kant admittedly was lacking in facts in order to also prove the reality of an intelligible consciousness next to the sensory one; but he believed in it, and although disappointed in the hope of finding the proof with Swedenborg, he wrote confidently though: "it will yet be proven in the future."

Kant thus suspected that an intelligible world of spirits existed, that the human soul belonged to it, that the earthly existence of living creatures was only incidental, that the simultaneous intelligible existence was the rule, and finally that the soul of the earthly human by virtue of its simultaneous intelligible nature could receive influences from the spirit world.

If the human were only earthly, then such an influence would be unthinkable on account of the total difference in nature of the two worlds, their inhabitants, and their ways of cognition. But if the human is simultaneously intelligible, then at least the possibility opens up of an intelligible influence at first on his intelligible soul so that it just becomes more about the further question of whether then such influences also pass over to the material human, to brain images and could thereby become known, which, expressed in modern language, would be possible by virtue of the moving of

---

†   Kant, "Träume eines Geistersehers, erläutert durch Träume der Metaphysik," 266–72.

*   Kant, 285–86.

xxvii

our threshold of perception. This psychological precondition is just as necessary as the metaphysical precondition cited by Kant; for since the latter, the simultaneity of the intelligible subject with the earthly person, is a constant, we must — if it alone should suffice — be constantly clairvoyant. But we are not always so; thus a temporary physiological precondition must be added to the constant metaphysical one, and the clairvoyance only occurs in conditions which are connected with the moving of the threshold of perception. Kant was not inclined to believe that the sleeping state offered opportunity for it:

"Certain philosophers believe without the slightest objection to be able to call on the state of being fast asleep when they want to prove the reality of vague imaginings, since nothing further of it is to be said with certainty than that we recall on awakening nothing of that which we might perhaps have had when fast asleep, and from that it only follows that those imaginings on awakening were not clearly imagined, and not that they were also vague at the time they were sleeping. I suspect rather that the same imaginings may be clearer and more expansive than even the clearest when awake; because this is to be expected with the complete relaxation of the outer senses by such an active being as the soul is, although since the body of the human is at the time not felt, on awakening the accompanying imagining lacks the same thing which could have helped the previous state of thought, as belonging to the same person, to achieve consciousness. The actions of a few sleepwalkers, which now and then show in such states more reason than usual, although they recall nothing of it on awakening, confirms the possibility of what I suspect of the state of being fast asleep. The dreams, by comparison, that is, the imaginings of the sleeping person which he recalls on awakening, do not belong here. For then the human is not completely asleep; he feels to a certain degree clearly and weaves his spirit's actions into the impressions of the outer senses. Hence he recalls them afterwards in part, but also finds in them utterly wild and tasteless chimeras, as they must then be

xxviii

necessarily, since in them ideas of imagination and those of the outer sensations are thrown amongst each other."[*]

This suspicion of Kant that exactly the valuable, non-physically conditioned dreams of deep sleep are followed by lack of memory, and that we have in them clearer and more expansive imaginings than even when awake, has been confirmed glowingly by somnambulism. Kant also indicates, however, in the above words the consequence which I drew in the "Philosophie der Mystik" [Philosophy of Mysticism], that such imaginings belong to the transcendental subject.

Such imaginings are certainly devalued to an extent by the transition into the brain, which also makes possible the subsequent recall, because they are then clothed in the sensory forms of cognition.

> "This disparity of the spiritual imaginings and those which belong to the corporeal life of the human must meanwhile not be seen as such a great hindrance to becoming conscious now and then even in this life of the influences from the side of the spirit world. For they cannot indeed pass over directly into the personal consciousness of the human, but yet pass over in that they animate according to the law of socialising concepts those images which are related to them, and awaken analogous imaginings of our senses which are probably not the spiritual concept, but its symbol anyway. For it is always just the same substance which belongs as a part both of this world and of the other, and both sorts of imaginings belong to the same subject and are linked to one another."[†]

Since now, however, spiritual sensations which our transcendental subject delivers, and which other spirits might deliver through the mediation of the same, with the transition into consciousness "are transfigured into shadow figures of sensory things" and "are woven directly into the fantasy of the imagination", it is thus impossible to distinguish the true

---

[*]   Kant, 285–86.
[†]   Kant, 286–87.

from the deceptions of the imagination. Since furthermore the condition of the visionary presumes an "unusually high sensitivity" and "an altered balance of the nerves", this condition can thus also indicate "a real illness"; finally it would also not be odd if such a visionary, because he was incapable of distinguishing true and false in the jumble of his imaginings, were at the same time a dreamer and, with this drawing in of strange imaginings into the outer sensations, "wild chimeras and strange grimaces were concocted".[*]

Kant now convinced himself of that when he read Swedenborg's writings. Swedenborg's belief in spirits is an entirely naive one. He has no idea that the transformation of spiritual imaginings into physical, i.e. transcendental ideas into ideas of the brain, only gives them an allegorical and symbolic value. Swedenborg considered all his visions to be true *sensu proprio* [in one's own sense]; for that reason Kant was completely disappointed — as will the present-day reader indeed be — and found in them only chimeras and fantasies.

According to the principles set forth by Kant, it is nonetheless to be distinguished between the content of the visions — which can be entirely worthless — and the transcendental-psychological basic condition for the possibility of receiving spiritual influences which according to Swedenborg consisted in that we belong simultaneously to two worlds. Kant not only did not reproach this theory of Swedenborg, but rather emphasised that it was the same as his own metaphysical ideas; for which reason he even protested quite seriously over the suggestion of plagiarism[†]. I thus do not want to defend Swedenborg's visions in the following, but rather simply his theory, which Kant acknowledged, as the following parallel texts might prove.

---

[*]   Kant, 288–90.
[†]   Kant, 334.

Kant.

The human soul would thus already have to be seen in the present life as connected with two worlds at the same time, of which it, in so far as it is bound to a personal unity with a body, clearly feels the material world alone, by comparison as a member of the spirit world receiving and giving the pure influences of immaterial nature so that as soon as that connection has stopped, the coexistence, in that it exists at any time with the spiritual nature, is alone leftover, and must present itself to its consciousness in clear view.[*]

It is accordingly as good as demonstrated, or it could easily be proven if you wanted to be long-winded, or yet better, it will in future, I know not where or when, yet be proven that the human soul also exists in this life in an indissolubly connected coexistence with all immaterial natures of the spirit world, that it alternately acts in this and receive from them impressions of which it is not conscious though as a human so long as everything is well[†].

Swedenborg.

The human was thus created so that it could be at the same time in the spirit world and in the natural world. The spirit world is where the angels are, and the natural world is where people are. And because the human was created thus, an interior and an exterior was thus given to him; the interior, whereby he can be in the spirit world, and the exterior, whereby he can be in the natural world. His interior is what the inner human is called, and the exterior is what his outer human is called.[‡]

[...] and yet the human is created thus that he cannot die with respect to his inner being[§].

And I must yet add to this that any human, so long as he lives in a body, is also with respect to his spirit coexistent with the spirits although he does not know it[**].

[‡] Emanuel Swedenborg, *Vom Neuen Jerusalem und dessen himmlichen Lehre: Nebst einem Vorbericht vom neuen Himmel und der neuen Erde*, 1772, § 25.

[§] Emanuel Swedenborg, "Die Ursachen, warum der Herr hat wollen auf unserer Erde, und auf keiner andern gebohren werden," in *Auserlesene Schriften*, 1st ed., vol. 3 (Frankfurt am Main: Christian Hechtel, 1776), 201.

[**] Emanuel Swedenborg, "Von der Geisterwelt un von dem Zustand des Menschen nach dem Tod," in *Auserlesene Schriften*, 1st ed., vol. 2 (Frankfurt am Main: Christian Hechtel, 1776), § 438.

---

[*] Kant, 275–76.
[†] Kant, 277.

It is accordingly indeed the same subject who belongs simultaneously as a member of the visible and the invisible world, but not just the same person because the ideas of the one, because of their different composition, are not attendant ideas of that of the other world, and hence what I think as a spirit is not recalled by me as a human, and vice versa [...] Incidentally the ideas of the spirit world may be as clear and lucid as you want, but this is not sufficient to be conscious of them as a human; how then even the idea of itself (i.e. of the soul) as a spirit will surely be obtained by deductions is with no human a transparent concept of experience.[*]

On the other hand it is also probable that the spiritual natures [...] could flow into the souls of the human as a being of the same nature, and also really mutually coexist every time with it, thus that in the communication [...] the concepts of the soul, as lucid ideas of immaterial things, cannot pass over into the clear consciousness of the human, at least not in their essential composition, because the materials for both ideas are of a different sort.[†]

For the human is in his being a spirit, and coexists at the same time with respect to his interior with the spirits; hence those to whom God has opened the interior can talk with them like one man with another, and this has been permitted to me daily for many years[‡].

From this it is clear that the human is created so that he, in that he lives on earth amongst humanity, should at the same time live in heaven amongst the angels; but because the human has become so corporeal, he has closed himself off to heaven[§].

That the human does not know that he is by nature among the spirits comes about because those spirits with which he coexists in the spirit world think and speak spiritually, but the spirit of the human, as long as it is in the material body, does so naturally, and the spiritual thinking and speaking cannot be understood nor perceived by the natural human[**].

---

[*]   Immanuel Kant, "Träume eines Geistersehers, erläutert durch Träume der Metaphysik," in *Imanuel Kant's vermischte Schriften*, vol. 2 (Halle: Regersche Buchhandlung, 1799), 285–86.

[†]   Kant, 277–78.

[‡]   Emanuel Swedenborg, "Von der Erden in dem Weltall," in *Auserlesene Schriften*, 1st ed., vol. 3 (Frankfurt am Main: Christian Hechtel, 1776), 81.

[§]   Emanuel Swedenborg, "Vom Himmel," in *Auserlesene Schriften*, 1st ed., vol. 1 (Frankfurt am Main: Christian Hechtel, 1776), 276.

[**] Emanuel Swedenborg, *Emanuel Swedenborgs Leben & Lehre: Eine Sammlung authentischer Urkunden über Swedenborgs Persönlichkeit, und ein Inbegriff seiner Theologie in wörtlichen Auszügen aus seinen Schriften* (Frankfurt am Main: Mittnacht, Since), 254.

Life with humans is twofold: the animal and the spiritual life. The animal life is the life of the human as human; and here the body is necessary so that the human lives. The other life is the spiritual life where the soul, independently from the body, must continue to exercise the same acts of life. For the animal life the body is necessary; there the soul is in connection with the body; it has an effect on the body and animates it. If now the machine of the body is destroyed, so that the soul can no longer have an effect on it; then indeed the animal life ceases, but not the spiritual.[*]

Since the soul is nothing else but the life of the human, but the spirit is the human itself, and the earthly body which it carries around in the world is only a serviceable tool whereby the spirit, which is the human himself, makes its proper effect on the natural world[†].

The human, seen in and of himself, is a spirit, and the corporeal which is added to it only because of the concerns of the natural world is only the tool of the spirit[‡].

The human, seen in and of himself, is a spirit, and also in the same form; for everything which lives and feels in the human befits his spirit, and in the human from his head to the soles of his feet there is not the least bit which does not have life and feeling; hence it now comes about that if the body is separated from its spirit, which is called dying, the human nonetheless remains a human and lives.[§]

---

[*]   See page 67 of the lectures below.

[†]   Emanuel Swedenborg, "Von der Hölle," in *Auserlesene Schriften*, 1st ed., vol. 2 (Frankfurt am Main: Christian Hechtel, 1776), 97-98 § 602.

[‡]   Emanuel Swedenborg, "Von der Geisterwelt un von dem Zustand des Menschen nach dem Tod," in *Auserlesene Schriften*, 1st ed., vol. 2 (Frankfurt am Main: Christian Hechtel, 1776), 185 § 435.

[§]   Emanuel Swedenborg, "Von der Geisterwelt un von dem Zustand des Menschen nach dem Tod," in *Auserlesene Schriften*, 1st ed., vol. 2 (Frankfurt am Main: Christian Hechtel, 1776), 183 § 433.

It happens accordingly in complete agreement with Kant and Swedenborg that I have expressed in my mystical writings the simultaneity of a transcendental subject with the earthly human in that I at first proved the psychological possibility of this simultaneity from the fact of the dramatic splitting of the ego in dream, but then proved it from the abilities of the hypnotised, somnambulists, and mediums[*]. With Kant, because he was not familiar with these facts, his findings were purely intuitive and all the more worthy of admiration; Swedenborg by comparison derived this simultaneity as the logical consequence from his own inner life.

Through that now the theory of the soul is steered onto entirely new tracks. Its emphasis is transferred from the consciousness into the unconscious. But this unconscious is with Kant not unconscious of itself, but rather only by the earthly human unconscious and is moreover individual. Kant thus disposes of materialism as well as pantheism.

But I can also now belatedly cite Kant in that I have sought the solution to the puzzle of humanity on the path of transcendental psychology. Kant said: "As little as empirical physics belongs to metaphysics, just as little" — he underlined the words *just as little* — "too does empirical psychology belong to metaphysics. For the theory of experience of the internal mind is the cognition of phenomena of the internal mind, just as bodies are phenomena of the external senses."[†‡] Thus only transcendental psychology is metaphysically usable. For that reason Kant also connected his metaphysical speculations over humanity with an investigation over a visionary. From that it arises that if Kant had ever written a philosophy of humanity it would have been a philosophy of mysticism. But when I wrote one such, my opponents knew precisely to show that already the entire foundation of my philosophy was deficient, and that I, in so far as I called on Kant, had misunderstood him!

---

[*] [Tr.: see Carl du Prel, *The Puzzle of Humanity: An Introduction to the Occult Sciences*, trans. Kerry Nitz (Auckland: K A Nitz, 2022)..]

[†] [Tr.: I have chosen to translate *den äussern Sinn* as external senses, but *den inneren Sinn* as inner mind, reflecting the multiple meanings of *Sinn*. Thus, inner mind can also be interpreted throughout as internal senses.]

[‡] See page 3 of the lectures below.

From the simultaneity of the transcendental subject with the earthly person there now result, however, deductively again consequences of a very remarkable sort which I have drawn in my mystical writings and concerning which I am now likewise in the position to cite Kant.

In his "Complete Works" admittedly, there is nothing of it. Kant only ever rarely stepped across the threshold of metaphysics. He indeed showed in his "Allgemeine Naturgeschichte und Theorie des Himmels" [Universal Natural History and Theory of the Heavens], in the "Gedanken von der wahren Schätzung der lebendigen Kräfte" [Thoughts on the True Estimation of Living Forces], and in the "Träume eines Geistersehers" [Dreams of a Visionary] his inclination to enter into metaphysical speculations over humanity; but with the deficiency in facts of experience he never ventured far in this direction and never forgot his main task because of it. He indeed knew that the metaphysicians, so long as each lives in a special world, each draws up a different system, can only be seen as dreamers, and that an end can only be brought to this anarchic state of philosophy by a "Critique of Pure Reason".

In one point, however, Kant also returns in this principle work of his, as well as in the "Practical Reason", to his mystical view of humanity. Already in the "Dreams" namely, Kant sees in the moral drive a proof for the intelligible nature of humanity. Ethics is to him a chapter of metaphysics and he protests against the superficial explanation of ethics from a (perhaps developed from Darwinian ideas) moral feeling whereby ethics would be transformed into mere empirical psychology. The moral drive which is effective in us as "an alien will" and "as a hidden force compels us to direct our intention at the same time to the welfare of others or at the mercy of strangers" appears to him as an outflow from a world whose beings are bound to a "moral unity". "Because the moral of the act relates to the inner state of the spirit, it can thus naturally only draw to itself in the immediate community of the spirits the act adequate to the entire morality. It would thereby occur now that the soul of the human must already in this life occupy its position among the spiritual substance of the universe according to its moral state."[*]

This derivation of ethics from the intelligible nature of humanity is something we also find in the "Critique of Pure Reason". In the presentation of the third antinomy "Möglichkeit der Causalität durch Freiheit in Vereinigung mit dem allgemeinen Gesetz der Naturnotwendigkeit" [Possibility of causality through freedom in union with the general law of natural necessity], Kant explains that we must ascribe to the human, who as moral being is subordinate in respect to all his actions to the law of natural necessity, next to his empirical character an intelligible character which, because it does not belong to the earthly phenomena, is to be seen as free, but can only be deduced, i.e. is just intelligible. The empirical character is the temporally emergent phenomenon of the intelligible character. "Thus freedom and nature would then, each in its complete meaning with just the same action after you compare them with their intelligible or sensory cause, be found at the same time and without any conflict."[†] It is not permitted to exclude human actions from the natural laws of causality, they are just as much subordinate to them as any other phenomenon of the sensory world; every action is the necessary product of motive and character. But empirical causality itself is only the phenomenon of a non-empirical, intelligible causality. "In this way the acting subject would, as *causa phaenomenon* [cause of the phenomenon], be chained with nature in inseparable dependency of all its actions, and only the *noumenon*[‡] of this subject (with all causality of the same in the phenomenon) would contain certain conditions which, if you want to rise from the empirical object to the transcendental, must be seen as merely intelligible."[§] In light of the intelligible character we are thus responsible for our actions; in the natural sciences' explanation of humanity by comparison there is neither freedom nor responsibility, thus

---

[*]   Kant, "Träume eines Geistersehers, erläutert durch Träume der Metaphysik," 280–82.

[†]   Immanuel Kant, *Kritik der reinen Vernunft*, ed. Karl Kehrbach (Leipzig: Reclam, 1877), 434.

[‡]   [Tr.: noumenon is the thing as it is in itself rather than as it is knowable by the senses.]

[§]   Kant, *Kritik der reinen Vernunft*, 435–37.

no morals, which are only possible when we assume a transcendental subject.

We find these same views in the "Critique of Practical Reason". There Kant also declares freedom and morals to be inseparable concepts. He also reproaches there the explanation of ethics from empirical psychology and declares freedom to be a "transcendental predicate", so that freedom thus draws after itself the "opening of an intelligible world". By comparison the mere psychological freedom on which empiricists think to ground morals is at base no better "than the freedom of a pot mixer which, if it is ever wound up, performs its motions by itself." The human who watches himself in his sensory self-awareness recognises the necessity of his actions, and there is so little to doubt in this that "if it were possible for us, in a human way of thinking as it shows itself both through the inner and the outer actions, to have such deep insight that any, even the slightest motive were known to us, likewise all outer causes affecting this, you could work out the behaviour of a human in the future with certainty, just like an eclipse of the moon or sun, and nevertheless claim with it that the human was free." The same being which knows itself to be sensorily integrated into the chain of natural necessity is though on the other hand "conscious as a thing in itself", thus knows itself to be free as an intelligible being. We have no view of this intelligible subject, but "in the absence of this view moral law assures us this difference of the relations of our actions as phenomena to the sensory being of our subject, of that by which this sensory being itself is related to the intelligible substratum in us."[*] Finally, Kant also expresses in his "Metaphysik der Sitten" [Metaphysics of Morals] that the moral will in us is the will of our transcendental subject.

To all attempts of modern times to derive morals from the sensory order of things, to transform the metaphysics of that into empirical psychology, Kant would object that morals and the intelligible world stand and fall together, that thus the naturalists who think they are permitted to use the word morals are at base illogical. In fact, if we were only sensory be-

---

[*]   Immanuel Kant, *Kritik der praktischen Vernunft*, ed. Karl Kehrbach (Leipzig: Reclam, 1878), 113, 114, 118, 120.

ings, we would be acting illogically to endeavour to be moral, but instead would have every right to follow the voice of egotism exclusively. Kant said: "If now the human assumes another world; then he must also arrange his actions according to it, otherwise he is acting like a rascal. But if he does not assume the other world; then he would be acting like a fool if he wanted to arrange his actions to conform to the law which he understands through reason; for then the worst rascal would be the best and cleverest in that he sought only to promote his happiness here because he cannot hope for any future happiness."[*] To a morality which furthers our own transcendental wellbeing now you can admittedly make the reproach of transcendental egotism — as Hartmann has reproached me — but Kant does not object to it in the least because he just knows that indeed the earthly egotism, but not the transcendental, is contradictory to the wellbeing of others.

"If I behave in conformance with the moral laws and make myself worthy of happiness, then I should also arrive at the possession of this happiness. But that does not happen. The moral laws lack this driving force; they carry no such promise. Without such driving forces, however, they are only grounds for determination, not though for execution; they are objectively practical, but not subjectively practical. I understand well the condition under which a freely acting being can be worthy of happiness, but I have not become aware that a being, when it has behaved thus that it is worthy of happiness, is under this condition *also really blessed with that*. If you cannot, however, hope for that, the rules of custom also have no driving power; for no creature can be indifferent with respect to the point of happiness; this is in accordance with the nature of any creature. The moral laws are thus indeed correct with respect to determination, but practically empty with respect to the execution. They have indeed, according to the understanding, a moving power of pleasure and displeasure, but *they have no driving power if they are not connected to*

---

[*]   See page 70 of the lectures below.

happiness. [...] It must accordingly be a promise to be really blessed with happiness if you have made yourself worthy of it."[*]

Moral laws would thus according to Kant remain nice theories without transcendental egotism, but never have driving power, which is what it comes down to though. But Kant bumps up against *this* egotism so little that he even derives from it the existence of God, indeed lets the last aim of the world coincide with it[†].

Thus then Kant throughout all his periods of development remained true to the assumption of a transcendental subject, although he could demonstrate it only from a single fact, the moral laws within us.

The transcendental subject is now, however, the foundation pillar, the logical prerequisite for all mysticism. Its acknowledgement, however, leads to consequences which I am capable of drawing all the more easily as yet other mystical facts than those of ethics are familiar to me. I was compelled on my own account to draw these consequences which result from the simultaneity of the transcendental subject with the earthly person, because I was of the forgivable opinion that Kant's collected works were complete. That I reaped those thanks for it which anyone reaps who bumps up against the fashion in thought was foreseeable, but could not lead me astray because in our days an absolutely baseless ignorance in matters of mysticism reigns, and indeed precisely in scientific circles whose disparaging judgement could thus be extremely indifferent to me.

But I was all the more surprised when I finally got hold of an exemplar of Kant's "Vorlesungen über Metaphysik" [Lectures on Metaphysics] to find in it the same consequences drawn, and indeed partly with such agreement that, if this form would not appear too pretentious to me, I could now deliver an entire series of parallel texts as I did above for Kant and Swedenborg. If I considered it worth the effort, I could

---

[*]   Immanuel Kant, *Immanuel Kant's Vorlesungen über die Metaphysik: nebst einer Einleitung, welche eine kurze Uebersicht der wichtigsten Veränderungen der Metaphysik seit Kant enthält*, ed. Karl Heinrich Ludwig Pölitz (Erfurt: Keysersche Buchhandlung, 1821), 290–92.

[†]   Kant, 291, 343.

now gloat over the embarrassment of my opponents who must either take back their contemptuous judgement of my mysticism or — in the case that they maintain it — include the philosopher Kant in that judgement.

We have seen that the transcendental subject was for Kant definitely in his pre-critical, in his critical, and in his post-critical periods. What consequences now result, however, from this assumption?

At first I drew one consequence which I have given various expressions: self-awareness does not exhaust itself in its object — we extend beyond our self-awareness — we are only immersed with a part of our being in the earthly order of things. This is also Kant's opinion, and branching off from the usual expression "intelligible subject", he even justifies my usage in that he said that "the transcendental subject is empirically unknown to us."[*] But this agrees again with the words of Swedenborg: "Over this I may yet add that any one person, so long as he lives in his body, is also with respect to his spirit coexisting with the spirits whether he directly knows it or not."[†]

Kant also expressed the same view in the "Dreams":

> "The idea which the soul of the human has of itself as a spirit through an immaterial viewing, in that it considers itself in relationship to beings of similar nature, is quite different from that, since its consciousness imagines itself as *human* through an image which has its origin in the impressions of corporeal organs and which is imagined in relationship to nothing else but material things. [...] Incidentally the ideas of the spirit world may be as clear and vivid as you like, but this is not sufficient to become conscious of it as a human; as then even the idea of his own self (i.e. the soul) as a spirit is probably acquired through deductions, but is with no human an observed or experienced fact."[‡]

---

[*] Kant, *Kritik der reinen Vernunft*, 437.

[†] Emanuel Swedenborg, "Vom Himmel, 2. Teil," in *Auserlesene Schriften*, 1st ed., vol. 2 (Frankfurt am Main: Christian Hechtel, 1776), 188 § 438.

[‡] Kant, "Träume eines Geistersehers, erläutert durch Träume der Metaphysik," 285–86.

Now because according to Kant our subject is empirically unknown to us, can only be deduced through the mind, but cannot be subjectively experienced, he calls it intelligible in contrast to sensory. But you can also call it transcendental in so far as it is hidden from our consciousness, indeed is not in itself unconscious, but is unknown to the human.

If the earthly human is the representation of a transcendental substratum, then the question arises of how the earthly differences of the human are grounded transcendentally. The solution to this question — which could result in a metaphysical Darwinism — was rejected by Kant: "But why the intelligible character gives just these phenomena and this empirical character under present circumstances exceeds all the capabilities of our mind to answer; indeed all authority of it just to ask."[*]

It is thus the rule that transcendental ideas cannot occur in sensory consciousness. I have indicated the exceptions to this rule in the states of deep sleep, of somnambulism, and of mediumism in which the physiological characteristic of a movement of the threshold of perception is common. Kant, for whom this area of facts was unfamiliar, could thus at most admit the possibility of such exceptions, and he admits them:

> "This disparity of spiritual imaginings and of those which belong to the corporeal life of humanity must not meanwhile be seen as such a great hindrance that it prevents all possibility of being conscious from time to time of the influences from the side of the spirit world even in this life. For they cannot indeed pass directly over into the personal consciousness of the human, but yet can in that they animate according to the law of socialising concepts those images which are related to them, and awaken analogous ideas of our senses which are probably not the spiritual concept itself, but its symbols. For it is always just the same substance which belongs as a member of both this world and of the other,

---

[*]   Kant, *Kritik der reinen Vernunft*, 444.

and both sorts of ideas belong to the same subject and are tied up with one another."[*]

From that Kant even wanted to explain that with the felt presence of a spirit this must reveal the image of a human figure, and said: "These sorts of phenomena can nonetheless not be something common and usual, but rather only happen with persons whose organs have shown an unusually great sensitivity."[†] To these abnormal humans of which Kant spoke, whose threshold of perception has permanently shifted, I have added the normal humans in abnormal circumstances with a momentary shift of the threshold of perception — the somnambulists. But without denying those sorts of spirit phenomena of which Kant spoke, and which you could call objectively caused hallucinations, I had to — because the facts of photographable phantoms is well-known — admit yet a second form of spirit phenomenon, with which then the portrayal of a human figure is only to be explained by the organising power of the soul.

Now because Kant at least admits the possibility of the transfer of transcendental ideas into sensory consciousness, he was also not ashamed to investigate the case of Swedenborg. The abilities namely which rumour ascribed to this visionary corresponded exactly to those which Kant associated with his concept of a simultaneously spiritual and corporeal being. He said that we would "draw out astonishing consequences" even if only *one* such occurrence could be assumed to be proven[‡]. These astonishing consequences now are, however, just those which he had already drawn, even before hearing of Swedenborg, but which he wanted to see as "dreams of metaphysics" so long as the proof of experience was lacking.

His reading of the writings of Swedenborg admittedly had the consequence that he called him a fantasist. But even if the content of Swedenborg's visions led and entitled him to that, he thought differently of the premise of these visions, namely

---

[*]   Kant, "Träume eines Geistersehers, erläutert durch Träume der Metaphysik," 286–87.

[†]   Kant, 288.

[‡]   Kant, 250.

of the dual nature of humans. Kant could not include this in his unfavourable judgement over Swedenborg because he would otherwise have had to call himself a fantasist and an insane person; for his own speculations over human nature agreed exactly with Swedenborg's theory. We will thus have to assume that Kant, even after he relinquished Swedenborg, hung onto his favourite idea, and even though waiving experience, he pictured to himself those "astonishing consequences" which result from the dual nature of humans. I will now deliver the proof of this claim.

What are these "astonishing consequences"? Firstly it is clear that with the Kantian-Swedenborgian view of humanity birth and death contain a quite different significance than is usually attached to them. If we are only immersed with one part of our being in the earthly order, but belong as intelligible beings to an intelligible world, then neither is birth our beginning, nor death our end. There were thus immediately the two problems: pre-existence and immortality. Both must be unavoidably answered in the affirmative if there is to be simultaneity of the earthly human with the transcendental subject.

To some Kantians it will now indeed sound odd when I say Kant taught pre-existence. But it is so, and his lectures do not allow the slightest doubt over that. In a remarkable place of the lectures on psychology he defined life as the binding of the soul with a body. Birth is the beginning, and death is the end of this connection. Birth and death are just states of the soul, thus assume the prior and following existence of the soul. Before birth the soul is in the same spiritual state in which it returns to again through death. By its binding to a body it gets into a cave, into a prison cell, whereby it is hindered in its actual spiritual life*.

The material birth is thus according to Kant only a reduction of our being in so far as we set aside for the duration of the life the transcendental capabilities; for the continuing transcendental subject, however, life is a gain since it previously had no consciousness of the sensory world and its self as human, but sucks up the acquisition of life.

---

*   See page 65 of the lectures below.

Now with respect to death, Kant had already concluded in the "Dreams" from the simultaneity of our dual being that:

> "If then finally through death the communion of the soul with the corporeal world is abolished, the life in the other world would only be a natural continuation of that association in that it had stood with it already in this life, and the entire consequences of the morality exercised here would again find itself in the actions which a being standing in indissoluble communion with the spirit world has already exercised there previously according to pneumatic laws. The present and future would thus as it were be of one piece, and make a constant whole, itself according to the *order of nature*."[*]

Death is thus with Kant an elevation of the individuality in the same sense as I expressed it in the closing chapter of my "monistischen Seelenlehre" [Monistic Theory of the Soul]: for the human, in so far as his soul leaves the earthly "prison cell", the "cave"; for the transcendental subject itself, however, by virtue of the sucking up of the earthly acquisitions. "For since the body is lifeless matter; it is a hindrance to life. [...] If now, however, the body ceases completely; then the soul is freed from its hindrance and only now does it begin to live properly. Thus death is not the absolute abolition of life, but rather a freeing of the hindrance to a complete life."[†]

Experience teaches only the death of the corporeal human. "No opponent can thus invent an argument from experience which demonstrates the mortality of the soul. Thus the immortality of the soul is at least secured against all objections which are derived from the experience."[‡] The positive proof follows from the nature of the transcendental subject which, bound with the material body only temporarily, is also not affected by its dissolution.

In the mystical world view the transcendental condition appears as the rule, and human life only as a temporary exception; life is accordingly a greater puzzle than death. Kant

---

[*]   Kant, "Träume eines Geistersehers, erläutert durch Träume der Metaphysik," 282–83.
[†]   See page 68 of the lectures below.
[‡]   See page 72 of the lectures below.

inclines to this view already in the "Dreams", where he calls life as "a communion between a spirit and a body" something mysterious, and says:

> "This immaterial world can thus be seen as a whole existing for itself, whose parts stand among one another in mutual combination and community, also without the mediation of physical things, *so that this last relationship is contingent and only entitled to a few*, indeed, where it is also found, does not hinder that not just the immaterial beings, which act in one another through the mediation of matter, stand apart from this in a special and universal connection and exercise every time a mutual influence amongst each other as immaterial beings so that their relationship by means of matter is only contingent and rests on a special divine institution, that is on the other hand natural and indissoluble."[*]

If we think about the series of accidents which must occur in order to help our personality come into existence with its qualitative definiteness; our corporeal and psychic dependence on the composition of precisely these specific parents, who perhaps met through the purest accident, e.g. in a summer resort together, or were at least only accidentally born in the same place and got to know each other, found themselves drawn to one another for unconscious reasons and entered into their bond of marriage under the ease of accidental conditions, whereas disruptive conditions would have separated them; who then also obtained us amongst a greater number of children; if we consider in particular those accidents which play out with most illegitimate births, with their often criminal and tragic accompanying circumstances; if we on the other hand consider the accidents which can cause the death of the living being, be it a stray bullet in battle, a falling roof tile, the ignorance of the local doctor, or in a railway catastrophe the glass of wine of which the locomotive driver drank too much; if we furthermore consider the content of

---

[*]   Kant, "Träume eines Geistersehers, erläutert durch Träume der Metaphysik," 271–72.

life itself, illness, hardship, and the thousands of evils, the struggle with stupidity and coarseness which each has to lead who is even only about half an idea ahead of their generation — then we seem to be lacking any grounds for believing in a higher purpose for earthly existence. Under the materialist assumption, which makes the "His Majesty the accident" — as Frederick II said — the steerer of our destiny, life appears absurd, coarse, an outrageous deceit, and we could only be outraged by the wretchedness and callousness of such an institution.

But that only applies under the assumption that we were placed with our entire being in this natural order. If on the other hand the earthly life is only the dream of a transcendental subject, then possibly the earthly pessimism can lead into a transcendental optimism, even if we are incapable of realising it; we would then have had from such an existence at least those benefits which Grillparzer described in his play "Der Traum ein Leben" [The Dream, a Life]. You could certainly interject that just an absurdity exists in that we know nothing of that transcendental relationship; but this ignorance is just the prerequisite for us drawing from this earthly life the transcendental advantages, for that reason practical mysticism also cannot be our life task.

If earthly existence were the rule, and absolutely solely the single and unique form of our existence, then admittedly the pessimists would be right. But if this antecedent does not apply, and if the simultaneity of a transcendental subject with the earthly person is assured — and it is assured for anyone who also admits only a single fact of transcendental psychology — then it can be further speculated with Kant that: "Now no creature which is placed by birth into the world by means of the accidental decision of its parents can be destined for a higher aim and a future life. [...] Only we see on the other hand that the life of the soul does not rest on the accidental nature of the breeding of animal life; but rather that it has already lasted before the animal life, and thus its existence depends on a higher purpose. The animal life is consequently

xlvi

incidental, but the spiritual is not. The spiritual life could though persist and be exercised even if it were also united accidentally with the body."[*]

This view of Kant's, however, agrees again with that of Swedenborg: "The human is not born by the parents into the spiritual, but rather into the natural life."[†]

Kant even does without the proof from the transcendental abilities of the human — for which he was lacking the basis in experience — and infers a future existence from the presence of the higher abilities among the normal abilities of humans which extend far beyond the needs of this life and are not capable of being given full expression in this one. Now even if this proof is of subordinate significance, I have presented it in the "monistic theory of the soul" and can now call not only on Kant's example, but rather can even mention that Kant clarified the proof through the same example as I did, in that I placed the concluding from the embryonic development of the human of his determination to enter into this world of light parallel to the concluding from our transcendental abilities of the future existence[‡].

What now concerns the composition of the future life, Kant himself equates to the condition before birth. But because we also do not stop being transcendental during the earthly life, this is in no way an interruption of the transcendental existence, but rather only a reduplication of existence. As with a meteorite the illuminated section of its path is only an accident, because that lies within our atmosphere, hence must not be observed in isolation, so too is our actual existence not interrupted by the entry into the earthly order and the life course illuminated by the earthly consciousness is also at the same time a part of a greater journey.

Certainly the comparison is no more justified in so far as it is not about a movement upon death to a spatial other side. I have described the other side as a mere other side to the threshold of perception, as a change in our forms of experience, and now find even in this point agreement with Kant:

---

[*]   See page 76 of the lectures below.

[†]   Emanuel Swedenborg, *Vom Neuen Jerusalem und dessen himmlichen Lehre: Nebst einem Vorbericht vom neuen Himmel und der neuen Erde*, 1772, § 148.

[‡]   See page 74 of the lectures below.

"The separation of the soul from the body is not to be set in a change of place. [...] But if the soul parts from the body; then it will not view the world as it appears, but rather as it is. Accordingly the separation of the soul from the body consists in the change of the sensory view into the spiritual view; and that is the other world. The other world is accordingly not another place, but rather just another view. The other world remains with respect to the objects the same world; it is not distinguished according to the substances; only it is viewed spiritually. [...] since the soul has through the body a view of the corporeal world; it will then, if it is freed from the sensory view of the body, have a spiritual view, and that is the other world. When you arrive in the other world; then you do not arrive in a community of other things, say on other planets; for with them I am already in connection, even if only in a more distant way; but rather you remain in this world, but have a spiritual view of everything. Thus the other world is not distinguished according to place from this one".[*]

Thus then Kant's definition of heaven also agrees with that of Swedenborg. The latter said: "From this light can now be shed on how the conditions and composition of the interior make heaven, and that heaven is in each one, but not outside him." ... "When heaven is revealed means when the inner sight, which is the sight of the spirit in the human, is revealed."[†]

I need not first say to my readers how much all the previous agrees with the detailed representations in my mystical writings, especially with the investigations over death and the conditions after death in the "monistic theory of souls". But the reproach that I did not understand Kant, I surely need not fear; for what Kant spoke for the abilities of comprehension of young students is absolutely not to be misunderstood. By contrast it remains the right of my opponents to deny me now the priority of my views. In this point I find myself in the pos-

---

[*]   See pages 77–79 of the lectures below.
[†]   Emanuel Swedenborg, "Vom Himmel," in *Auserlesene Schriften*, 1st ed., vol. 1 (Frankfurt am Main: Christian Hechtel, 1776), 32 §33, 185 §171.

ition of all post-Kantian philosophers, since in his writings lie the germ of development for all subsequent systems. Kant even thought an entire century ahead as a naturalist, just like he did as philosopher. But for that it is for me absolutely not to do with the fame of priority, I could not deliver a better proof at all than the treatise before you. But surely it is for me more to do with the matter namely of the mystical world view, because I consider it to be true, becoming established. That I will now in part in any case achieve through this proof that my views agree in all essential points with those of Kant, which I have demonstrated through citations. My writings have been condemned on the part of a few newspaper journalists, who do not even understand the titles of them, whereby I would have been astonished over their stupidity if I did not know that in part still much worse underlay it. These sorts of opponents, for whom I have now shown that their supposed blows hit at Kant, will now be somewhat more cautious, and even if they do not admit it, they will though see that my mystical views lie in the line of extension of Kantian philosophy.

You must have far too much time on your hands to investigate the question of whether Kant was a spiritualist. But if the question were put of whether he would be a spiritualist today, then I must answer this question in the affirmative. Firstly the case of Swedenborg would present itself to him more favourably today than at the time. Today the cases cited by Kant of Swedenborg's visionary gifts are more easily believed than at the time. The university librarian Tafel in Tübingen has delivered the proof in two texts* that in addition to the informants cited by Kant and Wieland for Swedenborg's visionary gifts, 20 others can be cited today; moreover that in addition to the facts mentioned by Kant, nine others of similar composition can be added. On, however, whether — as Tafel sought to prove — the letter to Miss von Knobloch was written later than the "Dreams", so that thus the less fa-

---

*   Johann Friedrich Immanuel Tafel, *Supplement zu Kant's Biographie und zu den Gesammt-Ausgaben seiner Werke* (Stuttgart: Becher & Müller, 1845); Johann Friedrich Immanuel Tafel, *Zwölf unumstössliche Erfahrungsbeweise für die Unsterblichkeit der Seele: Abriß des Lebens und Wirkens Emanuel Swedenborg's* (Stuttgart: Becher & Müller, 1845).

vourable judgement were absolved by a later more favourable one, does not matter at all anymore today. I need not get mixed up in this dispute at all; for it is indisputable that Kant's "Vorlesungen über Metaphysik" [Lectures on Metaphysics] are, according to Erdmann about 10 years, according to Poelitz about 20 years later than both that letter and the "Dreams". In these lectures, however, which were held over two, perhaps three semesters*, he called Swedenborg's theory sublime and gave a short portrayal of it†. He thus separates the visions of Swedenborg from the metaphysical premise which the latter gave for the possibility of such visions. Kant's ideas over the nature of humanity are in the "Lectures" still the same as in the "Dreams". He still taught the simultaneity of the transcendental subject with the earthly person.

Kant, who turned as far as Sweden in order to have the case of Swedenborg investigated, would today investigate the much nearer lying mystical facts. He would, unlike his colleagues, not allow himself to overlook hypnotism, somnambulism, and spiritualism, but would study them. With that he would then find the proofs of experience which he lacked for the correctness of his intuitions at the time.

Indeed Kant denied the possibility of simultaneous experiences from both worlds: "I cannot be at the same time in this and also in that world; for if I have a sensory view; then I am in this, and if I have a spiritual view, then I am in the other world; but this cannot occur at the same time."‡ But from the facts of somnambulism Kant would today acknowledge that both ways of experience, even if not simultaneous, can yet appear within the earthly life *alternately*, and arrive in the sensory consciousness. The point is that there are states of deep sleep in which the spiritual experience appears. Only when the sensory life is suppressed is the spiritual experience possible. To that extent you can compare the visionary gift with Kant to the gifts of Juno to Tiresias, making him blind so that she could provide him with the gift of prophesy, and can say,

---

*   Kant, *Immanuel Kant's Vorlesungen über die Metaphysik: nebst einer Einleitung, welche eine kurze Uebersicht der wichtigsten Veränderungen der Metaphysik seit Kant enthält*, V.

†   See page 79 of the lectures below.

‡   See page 81 of the lectures below.

"that the experiencing of knowledge of the other world can only be arrived at by forfeiting something of that understanding which you need for the present world."[*]

You can admittedly only believe in spirits in the usual sense of the word, which spiritualism also assumes, if you see in the soul not only a thinking, but also an organising being. If the soul is the organising principle of the body, the human is best explained monistically, and this monistic theory of the soul is the logical premise for the possibility of spiritual phenomena; expressions which aim at that are admittedly found with Kant: "My soul is whole in the whole body and whole in each of its parts"[†], and it is "the *thinking* soul which we believe we feel above all in the brain."[‡] "The place of the soul in the brain which we imagine is only a consciousness of the closer dependency of the place in the body where the soul acts the most."[§] The organisational ability must admittedly also be granted to the animal soul, and Kant does not shy from this in any way: "Whatever in the world contains a principium of *life* seems to be of immaterial nature."[**] "Thus then the immaterial world would encompass firstly all created intelligences, of which a few are bound with matter to a person, but others not, moreover the experiencing subjects in all types of animal."[††] Gestures and facial expressions also point to the organising soul: "Many claim that all souls are all the same, and the differences of the diversity merely arise from the body. These are arriving at materialism. If we on the other hand place all power in the soul, then we arrive at Stahlianism. Stahl was a physician who claimed this. You cannot completely contradict this opinion, for all characteristics of the soul are already to be read in the demeanour and the features of the body; thus the soul must have placed its characteristics into the body. A few claim that it itself also makes its body."[‡‡]

---

[*]   Kant, "Träume eines Geistersehers, erläutert durch Träume der Metaphysik," 291.

[†]   Kant, 262.

[‡]   Kant, 264.

[§]   See page 5 of the lectures below.

[**] Kant, "Träume eines Geistersehers, erläutert durch Träume der Metaphysik," 266.

[††] Kant, 275.

[‡‡] See page 41 of the lectures below.

Finally it sounds quite like Aristotle and in the sense of the monistic theory of souls when Kant says: "the body is only the form for the soul."* Also agreeing with that is that to him immortality is not perhaps a merely thinking existence: "Immortality is the natural necessity to live. [...] That proof, however, which is derived from nature and the concept of the matter itself, is every time the only possible proof, and it is transcendental."†

But now if the soul is organising, then admittedly there is the possibility that it also makes use of this ability after death, and with that we stand before the scorned spirit phenomena. Indeed still more so: our birth itself is then a spirit phenomenon, namely the representation of a transcendental subject in organic cellular matter. With that now the immediate thought is in any case that this incarnation is a voluntary one. But in any case the monistic theory of the soul arises actually by itself when you, like Kant, acknowledge in the soul not only the principle of thinking, but that of life.

If we now apply this to the spirit phenomena, Kant does not deny *a priori* any possibility of them. For him it is "just as much a stupid prejudice to believe without cause nothing of much which is told with some appearance of the truth, but to believe without examination everything of that which common rumour says"‡, and he says: "What philosopher has not once between the protestations of a rational and firmly convinced eyewitness and the inner resistance of an insurmountable doubt formed the most innocent figure you can imagine? Should he deny the correctness of all such spirit phenomena? What sort of reasons can he cite to disprove them?"§ "Just the same ignorance also result in that I do not dare to deny so completely all truth in the many stories of spirits, but with the usual, although strange reservation of drawing into doubt any single one, but attaching some belief to all taken together."**

---

*   See page 64 of the lectures below.
†   See page 66 of the lectures below.
‡   Kant, "Träume eines Geistersehers, erläutert durch Träume der Metaphysik," 250–51.
§   Kant, 250.
**   Kant, 308.

Even this modest confession of Kant's would be difficult for our current enlightenment; it has passed so far into its apodictic negations that for the reputation of this enlightenment retreat would be advisable; its scientific elation has also risen so much already that it has difficulty deciding on one and the same belief with old wives. We will thus have to wait some time yet for the noble confession that the old wives were always right, but the university wisdom was wrong. Meanwhile our enlightenment is of course not lacking in a scientific keyword with which it wants to set aside these uncomfortable spirits, and which pathology delivers to it: the hallucination.

Kant was far distant from such superficiality. He knew that spirit phenomena could not at all be struck from the field with the word "hallucination", because not two, but rather three possibilities are given, namely 1. the real phenomenon, 2. the empty fantasy of the seer, and 3. such phenomena with which "indeed only a deception of the imagination happens, but so that the cause of it is a truly spiritual influence which cannot be directly experienced, but rather only revealed to the consciousness through related images of the fantasy which assume the appearance of experiences."[*] This leads precisely to that distinction which I have raised between 1. real materialisations, 2. morbid hallucinations of the active fantasy, and 3. healthy hallucinations of the passive fantasy. Anyone who has learnt from hypnotism that in the brain of the hypnotised person any desired hallucination can be called forth — whereby thus the cause of the hallucination is not internal and pathological, but external — they will also not deny a spirit this ability to produce its image, hence carry out the above triplicity. Our medicine, however, lacks the concept of the healthy hallucination, and I know only of the psychiatrist Brière de Boismont who acknowledges it openly.[†]

At any rate Kant knew that in all ghost stories a lot of tricking of the senses occurs, the consideration of which has in it-

---

[*]   Kant, 288–89.

[†]   Alexandre Jacques François Brière de Boismont, *Des Hallucinations, ou Histoire raisonnée des apparitions, des visions, des songes, de l'extase, du magnétisme et du somnambulisme* (Paris: G. Baillière, 1845); Alexandre-Jacques-François Brierre de Boismont, *Hallucinations, or, The Rational History of Apparitions, Visions, Dreams, Ecstasy, Magnetism, and Somnambulism* (Philadelphia: Lindsay & Blakiston, 1853).

self the inconvenience of making his own suspicions over the duality of the human unnecessary[*]; he admitted furthermore that the scales of the mind are not entirely impartial in the judgement of the appearance of departed souls, and that all these stories "only weigh perceptibly in the scales of hope, but in conjecture seem to consist of pure air"[†]. The pre-critical Kant even calls the philosophical systems, because they contradict one another, dreams; he says that "we must be patient with the inconsistency of their visions until these gentlemen have finished dreaming"[‡], and because he still had the principal task of his life ahead of him, the replacement of the dogmatic philosophy with the critical, he spoke of his own metaphysical conjectures as a "fairy tale from the cloud cuckoo land of metaphysics."[§] But you can at most interpret such utterances, which stand opposite so many others, as symptoms of hesitation at the time of writing the "Dreams"; but it is entirely arbitrary while ignoring the other places to select them and to place the accent on them. But this has been done, and thus it has occurred that the "Dreams of a Visionary" is made out today almost generally to be a mere satire on the belief in spirits.

In contrast to this view, it must now be established, however, that in the lectures none of that hesitation is shown anymore. I thus certainly am correct to at least consider to be the true opinion of Kant that which he preserved over his critical period. But this is the simultaneity of the transcendental subject with the earthly person, and this is already certain for him because he cannot think of a morality without it. In this respect the "Dreams" and the lectures agree with the "Critique of Pure Reason", with the "Critique of Practical Reason", as with the "Metaphysik der Sitten" [Metaphysics of Morals]. Kant preserved the idea that "our fate in the future world may very much depend on how we have administered our posts in the present"[**] through all his periods.

---

[*]   Kant, "Träume eines Geistersehers, erläutert durch Träume der Metaphysik," 302.
[†]   Kant, 306.
[‡]   Kant, 292.
[§]   Kant, 316.
[**]   Kant, 346.

liv

The enlightened and mystics have cited Kant's "Dreams of a Visionary" for their own conflicting views. Which side the the greater right is on is thus not to be settled from that text. But when we compare it with the lectures, we recognise that the "Dreams" have been interpreted falsely by the Enlightenment; they at most show a hesitation of Kant which, however, has an end later in respect to the metaphysical key point. Since now I was led on a quite different path, namely that of the empirical experience from facts of modern times which I have gotten to know for the most part myself, to just that metaphysical key point, to the simultaneity of the transcendental subject with the earthly person — which the pre-critical, critical, and post-critical Kant preserves intact — it must thus at any rate not be improbable that I have correctly observed those facts and interpreted them correctly.

Let us sum up the forgoing. Kant taught:

1. Another world.
2. A transcendental subject.
3. The simultaneity of that with the earthly person.
   In that lies logically implicit:
   a. The insufficiency of self-consciousness for the knowledge of our being.
   b. The only partial immersion of this being in the material world.
4. Pre-existence.
5. Immortality.
6. Birth as incarnation of a transcendental subject.
7. Material existence as exception, the transcendental as rule.
8. The necessity of a transcendental psychology for the proof of the soul.
9. The voice of conscience as the voice of the transcendental subject.
10. The other side [that is, the hereafter] as merely the other side of the threshold of perception.

The mere possibilities to which Kant further admits, I can leave aside entirely. But if I were now called upon to draw out the quintessence from my own mystical writings, then I could not find a shorter expression than just the above summary to which my mysticism relates in the same way as a book to its table of contents. The reader of my writings will recognise everything from this miniature picture without doubt and will confess to me that I derived the above points from facts of experience, represented them in more detail, and connected them into an organic whole. Certainly Kant would be falsely defined if I were to thereby call him a mystical philosopher; but it is not to be denied that in his writings there is found strewn and in a germinal state everything which, united and brought into systematic connection, knits together into a mystical world view.

It is an unjustified high-handedness to want to see the true author only in one of his works, and that applies especially to philosophy; for there are indeed philosophers who did not deviate anymore from the keyword expressed once and for all, like e.g. Hegel; but with most a piece of the history of development of philosophy plays out within their own individuality. Even a Schopenhauer expressed in the last years of his life in his mystical essays — apparent intentionality in the fate of the individual, visionaries, magic, metaphysics of sexual love — views which only needed to be developed in order to transform his panthelism into individualism.[*] For that reason it is also high-handed to want to see the true Kant only in the "Critique of Pure Reason", even if it might also be the most characteristic work of this philosopher. Hence I have a right to collect and utilise the mystical seeds from all his writings. But were I to limit myself to his key work, then the simultaneity of the transcendental subject and the earthly human would also still remain then, only he would be limited there to the ethical motivation of this simultaneity. He claims there the intelligible freedom, and if this applies to any single act, then it must also apply to life itself and to the birth. Kant did not admittedly express this view directly, that the incarnation is the free act of the transcendental subject; but it lies in his premises.

There exists no contradiction between the "Critique of Pure Reason", which draws limits on the human spirit and denies it from penetrating in a reflective way into the intelli-

---

[*] An excellent representation of the mysticism of Schopenhauer can be found by the reader in the February issue of the "Sphinx" (1888) and in Raphael von Koeber, *Die Philosophie Arthur Schopenhauers* (Heidelberg: G. Weiss, 1888).

gible world, and the other writings which contain mystical components. Opposite all the dogmatic metaphysics, the "Critique" continued to apply. But if Kant despite his own interdiction offers us metaphysical views in the form of intuitions, and we investigate the sources from which they were drawn, then we will just find his metaphysical views of humanity confirmed again. Each intuition is an inspiration for the sensory consciousness because it thereby only shows passive receptivity. Such inspirations can now emanate from spirits on the other side or — which is of course much more probable — from the human on the other side, i.e. the transcendental subject; it is thus only possible — as Kant himself said — if we belong to both worlds. If anything is transcendental, then it is the instincts of animals and the intuitions of genius. Processes which run without our consciousness playing a part or whose mere end result falls into the consciousness are transcendental; to them belong not only the organic functions, but also the ingenious thoughts, only we are more accustomed to this phenomenon than to the in no way more wonderful one of clairvoyance, which is likewise the work of our transcendental subject. If you wanted, however, to explain this clairvoyance pantheistically, like e.g. Hartmann, then you would in the end be required to set the world substance in motion in all the cases of dreamt lottery numbers which come out, and that then means shooting at sparrows with cannons.

In Kant's time, you could counter metaphysical speculations like those I have attempted in my mystical writings with the critical Kant who gave his own intuitions as unprovable hypotheses. Today, however, the question stands quite differently and Kant himself would entertain these hypotheses of his still further because meanwhile the proofs of experience which he prophesied have appeared, mysticism has thus become an empirical science, but experience definitely decides. "Now since the rational causes in the same instances are to neither the invention, nor the confirmation of the possibility or impossibility of the least importance, you can concede only to the experiences the right of decision."* The day is already

---

* Kant, "Träume eines Geistersehers, erläutert durch Träume der Metaphysik," 342–43.

here which Kant prophesied with his words: "It will in future yet be proved that the human soul also stands in this life in an indissolubly tied community with all the immaterial natures of the spirit world."[*] Hypnotism and somnambulism show us the transcendental subject, spiritualism the alien subjects of this nature. It is thus an anachronism when my opponents counter me with Kant; he himself would disown them, since my mysticism is not assembled from intuitions, but instead rests on facts of experience. My experiences, however, cannot deprive me of my opponents; they do not have a monopoly on the field of facts alone, but rather I also possess my hunting maps.

To the scientific observation of mystical facts and their philosophical utilisation Kant would thus of course have no objection. To the contrary, he would probably despite his own mystical tendencies also not define in the sense of mysticism the practical tasks which he places on the human. The human has earthly tasks to fulfill in the earthly life, be it individually, or be it as a member of society. "In general we offer that it is not appropriate at all here for our destiny to worry much about the future world; but rather we must complete the circle to which we are destined here and wait to see how it will be in respect to the future world."[†] In order to fulfill transcendental tasks, we would not have assumed the earthly nature and Kant would say to the practical mystic that "the property of unwrapping the impressions of the spirit world in this life into clear views could hardly be of any use because as a result the spiritual perception is necessarily bound up so precisely in the fantasy of the imagination that it would have to be impossible to distinguish in it the true from the great deceptions which surround it."[‡] That applies to nine tenths of our mystical literature. Kant would, however, emphasise still more that the practical mysticism, because it is bound up with the lying fallow of normal reason, hinders us from developing

---

[*]   Kant, 277.

[†]   See page 81 of the lectures below.

[‡]   Kant, "Träume eines Geistersehers, erläutert durch Träume der Metaphysik," 289.

this; and it would "make the use of my reason impossible, and annul the conditions under which my reason can alone be used."[*]

You can concede to mysticism a high scientific value and yet dismiss the practice. Anyone who carries out practical mysticism revokes as an earthly person the intention from which his transcendental subject incarnated itself. Anyone who develops the transcendental way of perceiving and sensing at the cost of the earthly must logically presuppose that the limitation of our earthly consciousness to the earthly world is a failed institution which he must hardly succeed in proving; he must claim that the transcendental subject has ended up on the wrong track with the incarnation, and with his attempt to make this good again as an earthly human, he will sit himself between two chairs; for our brain which is open to earthly influences, if it were simultaneously flashed through by transcendental influences, would come up short in both directions. The transcendental way of cognition, even awoken to the highest achievable degree, would remain far behind the cognition of a real transcendental subject, since the hindrance of the body is never to be disposed of entirely. Under these conditions a transcendental being which voluntarily incarnated itself, but furthermore would use this earthly life at the cost of the normal use of reason to parade its transcendental nature, which though would succeed only very imperfectly — such a being would have done better to refrain from incarnation; it would be like that fool who amputates his healthy leg and has it replaced by a wooden leg, or a government minister who would take his retirement from the civil service in order to enter again as an intern with the ambition of becoming an articled clerk.

Hence I see more wisdom in the life rule of Arabs that the human should use life either to plant a tree, or rear a child, or write a book, than in all the practical prescriptions of the mystics, ascetics, and theosophers. I will also add: one does not hinder the other.

---

[*]   See page 81 of the lectures below.

Lectures on Psychology

Introductory Concepts

In the left-over parts of metaphysics* nature of a thing over-all was dealt with, and the objects were considered overall. In this consideration the nature signifies the epitome of all inner principles and all of that which belongs to the existence of the thing. But if you talk in general about the nature, it is thus only about the form, and then the nature does not signify any object, but rather only the way in which the object exists. — The nature is that in the existence which the being is in the concept. In cosmology one talks about the nature of anything overall, of the nature of the world, or the nature in general understanding where it signifies the embodiment of all natures; and then the nature is the embodiment of all the objects of the senses. This cognition of the objects of the senses is *physiology*. Now what is not any object of the senses goes beyond the nature and is hyperphysical. Accordingly the embodiment of all objects of the senses is nature, and the cognition of nature or physiology can be twofold: *empirical* and *rational*. This division of physiology, however, only applies to the form.

The *empirical* physiology is the cognition of the objects of the senses in so far as they are obtained from the principles of experience. The *rational* physiology is the cognition of objects in so far as they are not created from experience, but rather from a concept of reason. The *object* is always an object of the senses and experience; only the *cognition* of it can be arrived at through pure concepts of reason; for by that physiology

---

*　In the left-over parts Kant dealt with ontology and cosmology. (Ed. [du Prel])

1

distinguishes itself from transcendental philosophy where the object itself is borrowed not from experience, but rather from pure reason. Also belonging to *Physiologia rationalis* [rational physiology] will be, for example, that a body is divisible to infinity; for to the concept of the body belongs an entirety of matter. But matter takes up a space, and space is divisible to infinity; thus any phenomenon in space is too. To matter belongs moreover a certain lifelessness (*vis inertiae* [force of inertia]), whereby it distinguishes itself from the thinking being. Accordingly matter cannot move in any other way than by being driven by an external force. This all belongs to *Physiologia rationalis* and you can absolutely understand the entire theory of motion from the concept of the body. But that the bodies attract one another; that they are heavy; that bodies are fluid — all that can only be recognised from experience; consequently this belongs to *Physiologia empirica* [empirical physiology].

But physiology can also be classified with respect to the object or the material. Since physiology is a cognition of the objects of the senses, you will easily understand the classification if you notice that you have two kinds of senses, namely *external* senses and an *internal* mind*. Accordingly there is a physiology of objects of the *external* senses, and a physiology of objects of the *internal* mind. The physiology of the external senses is *physics*, and the physiology of the internal mind is *psychology*. Both parts, both physics and psychology, can, according to the previous classification, be twofold in form: empirical and rational. There is accordingly an empirical and rational physics and psychology. The general purpose of the act, or the general character of the object of the internal mind is *thinking*; and the general character of the object of the external senses is *moving*. In the *Psychologia generalis* [general psychology] it is thus overall about the thinking being, which is *pneumatology*; but in the *Psychologia speciali* [specialist psychology] it is about the thinking subject which we know and which is *our soul*. The objects of the external senses, or the bodies overall, are also dealt with in this way in

---

*　[Tr.: The German word *Sinn* can mean both sense and mind, and so the external has been translated here as sense and the internal as mind.]

the *Physica generali* [general physics], and the bodies we know in the *Physica speciali* [specialist physics]. *Psychologia empirica is the cognition of the objects of the internal mind, in so far as it is not drawn from experience. Physica empirica* is the cognition of the objects of the external senses, in so far as it is borrowed from experience. Rational psychology *is the cognition of the objects of the internal mind, in so far as it is borrowed from pure reason.* — As little as empirical physics belongs to metaphysics, *just as little too does empirical psychology belong to metaphysics.* For the theory of experience of the internal mind is the cognition of phenomena of the internal mind, just as bodies are phenomena of the external senses. Thus the same thing happens in the *Psychologia empirica* as happens in empirical physics; just that the material in the *Psychologia empirica* is given by the internal mind, and in empirical physics by the external senses. Both are thus theories of experience.

Metaphysics distinguishes itself thereby from physics and all theories of experience in that it is a science of pure reason, in contrast physics borrows its principles from experience. It is very good to define the boundaries of sciences and to understand the reason for divisions so that you have a system; for without this you are always an apprentice, and you do not know how the science, e.g. psychology, arrived at metaphysics, and whether it would not be possible that several sciences could be brought into it. Accordingly you see that the *Psychologia rationalis* and the *Physica rationalis* surely belong to metaphysics because their principles are borrowed from pure reason. The *Psychologia empirica* and the *Physica empirica*, however, do not belong in it at all.

The reason why the *Psychologia empirica* has been placed in metaphysics is probably this: you never rightly knew what metaphysics was, although it has been plied for so long. You did not know how to define its boundaries; hence you placed a lot in it which did not belong there; which rests on the definition in that you defined it by "the first principles of human cognition". But nothing at all now is defined thereby; for in all parts there is always a first. The second cause was probably this: the theory of experience of the phenomena of the soul has not arrived at any system so that it could have constituted a special academic discipline. If it would have been as large as empirical physics, then it would have isolated itself likewise from metaphysics by its vast extent. But because it is small, and you did not want to leave it out entirely, you shoved it in metaphysics onto rational psychology; and the usage was not so soon got rid of. But now it is already very large, and it will almost have arrived at such a size as empirical physics. *It also deserves to be presented just as particularly as empirical physics*; for the cognition of the human is the equal of the cognition of the body; indeed it is far preferred to the latter in its value. If it becomes an academic science, then it will be in the position to arrive at its full extent; for an academic teacher has more practice in the sciences than a guild-free scholar. The former is more likely to understand the gaps and the unclear parts by the frequent presentation of them, and has with every new lecture the new determination to improve on such. *Just such journeys will accordingly be made in time to discern humanity as were made to get to know plants and animals.*

Psychology is thus a psychology of the internal mind or the thinking being, just as physics is a physiology of the external senses or the corporeal being. I consider the thinking being either merely from concepts, and that is the *Psychologia rationalis*; or by experience, which happens partly internally in myself, or externally, which I perceive in other natures, and recognise according to the analogy which they have with me; and that is the *Psychologia empirica*, where I consider thinking natures through experience. The substratum which lies at the base, and which expresses the consciousness of the internal mind, is the *concept of the ego* which is merely a concept of empirical psychology. The sentence *I am* was assumed by *Descartes* to be the first statement of experience which is evident; for I could have the idea of the body even if no body were there; but when I look at myself, I am directly conscious of me. I am, however, not conscious of the existence of all things external to me, rather only of the idea. But it does not follow that such ideas must always be based on things too, they are only analogous cases of experience; I infer existence from experience. This *ego* can be taken in a dual sense: *the I as human*, and *the I as intelligence*. I, *as a hu-*

man, am an object of the *internal* mind and *external* senses. I, *as an intelligence*, am an object *of the internal mind alone*; I do not say I am a body, but rather what is on me is a body. This intelligence which is bound up with the body and constitutes the human is called *soul*; but *considered alone* without the body it is called intelligence. The soul is thus not merely thinking substance, but rather is to the extent it constitutes a unity bound with the body. Accordingly the changes of the body are my changes.

I *as soul* am determined by the body, and stand in commerce with the latter. I as *intelligence* am in no place; for place is a relation of the external experience; as intelligence, however, I am not an external object which can be defined in view of relations. My place in the world is defined thus by the place of my body in the world; for what appears and shall stand in external relation must be a body. I will thus not be able to directly determine my place, but rather I as soul determine my place in the world through my body; but I cannot determine my place in the body, for otherwise I would have to be able to view myself in an external relation. *The place of the soul in the brain* which we imagine is only a consciousness of the closer dependency of the place in the body where the soul acts the most. It is an analogy of the place, but not its position. Already the bare consciousness gives me the difference of soul and body; for the external thing which I see on me is obviously different from the thinking principle in me; and this thinking principle is different again from all that which can only be an object of the external senses.

A human whose body has been torn open can see his entrails and all his inner parts; thus *this* internal thing is merely a corporeal being and entirely different from the thinking being. A human can lose many of his limbs, despite which he still remains and can say: I am. The foot belongs to him. But when it is sawed off, then he sees it just like any other thing which he cannot use anymore, like an old boot which he must throw away. But he always remains himself unchanged, and his thinking ego loses nothing. Thus everyone understands easily, even the basest mind, that they have a soul which is different from their body.

The mere concept of the ego which is unchangeable, which you cannot even describe anymore in so far as it expresses the object of the internal mind and distinguishes it, is the foundation of many other concepts. For this concept of the ego expresses:

1. The substantiality. — Substance is the first subject of all inherent accidents. This ego, however, is an absolute subject to which all accidents and predicates can belong, and which can not be a predicate of any other thing. Thus the ego expresses the substantial; for that substratum which adheres to all accidents is the substantial. This is the only case where we can directly see the substance. We cannot see the substratum and the first subject of any thing; but in me I see the substance directly. The ego thus expresses not only the substance, but also the substantial itself. Indeed still more, the concept which we have overall of all substances, we have borrowed from this ego. This is the original concept of substances. — This concept of the ego expresses:

2. The *simplicity* that the soul which thinks in me constitutes an absolute unity, a *Singulare in sensu absoluto* [singular in the absolute sense], and thus the simplicity; for many substances cannot together constitute a soul. — Many cannot indeed say I, this is thus the strictest singularity. — Finally, this concept of the ego also expresses:

3. The *immateriality*. The reason that humans thought of themselves as spiritual beings is the analysis of themselves. It occurred by the analysis of that which they thought when they imagined themselves as objects of the internal mind; for with respect to their consciousness it would have to be enlightening to them that this was not an object of the external senses. But that which is not an object of the external senses is immaterial. — Something is *immaterial*, however, when it is present in space without taking up a space, and without being impenetrable.

I as intelligence am a being which thinks and which wants. *The thinking and wanting can, however, not be seen*; thus I

6

am also not an object of the external view. But that which is not an object of the external view is immaterial. This serves me in so far as this main category proves the consciousness of a subject which is different from the body, thus proves a soul; therefore we can already speak in this respect of a soul. I am conscious of two objects:

1. my subject and my condition;
2. the things external to me.

My imagination is either directed at objects or at myself. In the first case I am conscious of other findings; in the second case of my subject. E.g. a human who calculates then is conscious of the numbers; in the time in which he calculates, however, not conscious of his subject at all. This is the *Conscientia logica* [logical consciousness] which differs from the *Conscientia psychologica* [psychological consciousness] where you are conscious only of your subject. The *objective* consciousness, or the cognition of objects with consciousness, is a necessary condition of having a knowledge of all objects. The *subjective* consciousness is, however, a violent condition. It is an observation turned in on oneself; it is not discursive, but rather intuitive. The healthiest condition is the consciousness of external objects. But the condition of perception or of consciousness of oneself is also necessary, and indeed necessary as a revision. The consciousness is a knowledge of that which applies to me. It is an idea of my ideas, it is a self-awareness, perception. With regard to the objective consciousness, those ideas which we have of the objects are called *clear* ideas of which you are conscious; *distinct* ideas of whose characteristics you are also conscious; and *obscure* ideas of which you are not at all conscious. Actually this difference belongs to logic. As far as pertains to psychology, it is to be noted here that there are obscure ideas. Leibniz said: the greatest treasure of the soul consists of obscure ideas which only become distinct through the consciousness of the soul. If we might become conscious of all our obscure ideas and of the entire extent of the soul at once directly by a supernatural circumstance, then we might be astonished over ourselves, and over the treasure in our soul, and what wealth it contains in the way of knowledge of itself. When we direct our eyes through a telescope to the most distant heavenly bodies, then the telescope does nothing more than awake in us the consciousness of innumerable heavenly bodies which cannot be seen with the naked eye, but which already lay darkly in our soul. If the human were able to be conscious of all that which he perceives of bodies through microscopes, then he would have a great knowledge of the bodies which he also now already really knows, only he is not conscious of that. Furthermore, everything which is taught in metaphysics and ethics everybody knows already; only they were not conscious of it; and the person who explains to us and lectures us on such actually tells us nothing new which we would not have known, rather they only make me conscious of what was already in me. If God were at once to directly bring light into our souls so that we could be conscious of all our ideas, then we would see all heavenly bodies quite clearly and distinctly, just as if we had them before our eyes. If accordingly in future life our souls will be conscious of all our obscure ideas, then the most learned will not get further than the most unlearned, only the learned is already conscious here of something more. But if in both souls a light goes up, then they are both equally clear and distinct. There thus lies in the field of obscure ideas a treasure which constitutes the deep abyss of the human knowledge which we cannot reach.

Of the General Division of Intellectual Capabilities

I feel either like I am *suffering* or *self-regulating*. That which belongs to my capabilities to the extent I am suffering belongs to my lower capabilities. That which belongs to my capabilities to the extent I am active belongs to my higher capabilities.

Three things belong to my capabilities:

1. *ideas*;
2. *desires*; and
3. the *feeling of pleasure and displeasure*.

The *capability of ideas*, or the capability of knowledge, is either the *lower* capability of knowledge or the *higher* capability of knowledge. The *lower* capability of knowledge is a power of having ideas to the extent we are influenced by objects. The *higher* capability of knowledge is a power of having ideas from within ourselves.

8

The *capability of desire* is either a *higher* or a *lower* capability of desire. The *lower* capability of desire is a power of desiring something to the extent we are influenced by objects. The *higher* capability of desire is a power of desiring something from ourselves independently of objects. Likewise too the *capability of pleasure and displeasure* are a *higher* or *lower* capability. The *lower* capability of pleasure and displeasure is a power of finding a pleasure or displeasure in the objects which influence us. The *higher* capability of pleasure or displeasure is a power of feeling a pleasure and displeasure in ourselves independently of the objects. All lower capabilities make up *sensoriality*, and all higher capabilities make up *intellectuality*.

Sensitivity is a condition of objects of recognising something to the extent you are influenced by objects; and of desiring something, or having a pleasure or displeasure in something to the extent you are influenced by the objects. — *Intellectuality* is, however, a capability of imagination, of desire or the feeling of pleasure or displeasure to the extent you are entirely independent of the objects. Sensory knowledge is *not thereby* sensory because it is confused; but rather in that it takes place in the disposition to the extent that it is influenced by objects. Intellectual knowledge is in turn *not thereby* intellectual because it is clear, but rather because it springs from within ourselves. Accordingly intellectual ideas can be confused, and the sensory clear. Because of that, that something is intellectual does not mean that it is clear, and that something is sensory does not mean that it is obscure. Thus there is a sensory and an intellectual clarity. The sensory exists in contemplation, the intellectual in the concepts. Sensoriality is the passive characteristic of our capabilities of cognition to the extent we are influenced by objects. But intellectuality is the spontaneity of our capabilities to the extent we either recognise ourselves, or desire something, or have pleasure or displeasure in something. — The reason why Wolff and others consider confused knowledge to be sensory is this: because the knowledge, before it is worked on by the mind, has no clarity, instead the knowledge is still logically confused, i.e. when it cannot be understood by concepts. If now the knowledge is confused, then the reason is not because it is sensory, but rather because it is logically confused, and the mind has not yet worked on it. All knowledge which comes from the senses is at first logically confused if it has not yet been worked on by the mind; only because it is still confused does not make it sensory; rather when it is taken in from the senses, then it remains by its origin sensory, even if it is worked on by the mind and becomes clear. For clarity and obscurity are only forms which befit both sensory and the intellectual ideas. They are, however, sensory and intellectual by their origin; they may be clear or confused.

Of sensory capabilities of knowledge in detail

The sensory capabilities of knowledge contain those ideas which we have of the object to the extent we are influenced by them.

We distinguish, however, the sensory capabilities of knowledge into the capabilities of the senses themselves, and the emulated knowledge of the senses. The sensory knowledge arises either entirely from the impression of the object, and then this sensory knowledge is an idea of the senses themselves; or the sensory knowledge arises from the disposition, but under the condition under which the disposition is influenced by the objects, and then the sensory knowledge is an emulated idea of the senses. E.g. the idea of that which I see; furthermore the idea of the sour, the sweet, etc. are ideas of the senses themselves. But when I recall a house which I once saw, then the idea arises now from the disposition; but under the condition though that the senses were previously influenced by this object. Such sensory knowledge which arises from the spontaneity of the disposition is called *knowledge of the forming power*; and the knowledge which arises from the impression of the object is called *ideas of the senses themselves*.

You can also divide up sensoriality in the following way. All sensory knowledge is either *given* or *made*. To the given we can assign the senses overall, or the idea of the senses themselves. To the made we assign:

1. *facultatem fingendi* [faculty for fabrication];
2. *facultatem componendi* [faculty of composing];
3. *facultatem signandi* [faculty of naming];

To the *Facultas fingendi*, however, belong:
- *a)* *facultas formandi* [faculty for forming],
- *b)* *facultas imaginandi* [faculty of imagination],
- *c)* *facultas praevidendi* [faculty of foresight].

The *ideas of the forming power* are thus divided up:
1. into the forming power in itself, which is the *genus* [race];
2. into the reproductive power, *facultas formandi*;
3. into the power of emulation, *facultas imaginandi*;
4. into the power of foreknowledge, *facultas praevidendi*.

These powers all belong to the forming power of the sensory capabilities. This forming power which belongs to sensoriality is different from the thinking power which belongs to the mind.

Of the ideas of the senses themselves

The ideas of the senses themselves are possible to the extent we are influenced by objects. But we can be influenced in various ways by the objects; that is, the ideas of the objects which arise by impression are different from one another; e.g. taste is different from smell. In so far as the various senses have no similarity, we call them specific senses; hence we have five: seeing, hearing, smelling, tasting, and feeling. The reason that we have a certain number of senses is because we have a certain number of organs of the body through which we receive the impressions of objects, and thus we divide the senses according to the division of the organs of the body. But we also have yet other sensory perceptions for which we have no special organs, and which we thus cannot distinguish either; e.g. the feeling of hot and cold, of sound etc. is spread across our entire body. Because we thus do not have more than five organs, we also assume only five senses.

A few of these senses are objective, others subjective. The objective senses are connected with the subjective at the same time; thus the objective senses are not objective alone, but also subjective. Either the objective is greater with the senses than the subjective, or the subjective is greater than the objective. E.g. with sight the objective is greater than the subjective; and with the strong sound which penetrates into the ears the subjective is greater. But if we look not at the strength, but rather at the quality of the senses, then we notice that seeing, hearing, and feeling are more objective than subjective, but smell and taste are more subjective than objective senses. The subjective senses are senses of the conscience; the objective senses by contrast are informing senses. The informing senses are either fine, when they act on us in the distance by means of a fine material; or coarse, when they act on us and influence us by means of a coarse material. Thus the sense of vision is the finest, because the material of light by means of which the objects influence us is the finest. Hearing is somewhat coarser; but feeling is the coarsest. Vision and feeling are completely objective ideas. Feeling is, however, the fundamental one of the objective ideas; for by feeling I can perceive forms in that I can touch them on all sides; it is thus the art of interpretation of forms. By seeing I recognise only the surface of the object.

We do not have to believe that all knowledge of the senses come from the senses; but rather it also comes *from the mind* which reflects on the objects which are exposed to our senses, whereby we then receive the sensory knowledge. In such a way the *vitium subreptionis* [error of conflation of knowing and experiencing] arises with us; in that because we accustomed ourselves from youth to imagining everything through the senses, we do not notice the reflections of the mind over the senses, and consider the knowledge to be direct experiences of the senses.

The old philosophers, like Aristotle and after him the scholastics, said that all our concepts originate from the senses, which they expressed through the sentence: *nihil est in intellectu, quod non antea fuerit in sensu* [there is nothing in the mind which has not previously been in the senses]. The mind cannot recognise anything which the senses have not experienced previously. Here Aristotle spoke against Plato who as a mystical philosopher claimed the opposite, and not only the concept as innate, but also seen as such which remains of the last view of God, which the body now hinders us from. — Epicurus went too far again, and said all our concepts are concepts of experience of the senses. In order to recognise and understand clearly how far the sentence of

Aristotle can be allowed, you must limit the sentence some-what, and say: *nihil est quoad materiam in intellectu, quod non antea fuerit in sensu* [there is nothing as far as matter in the mind which has not previously been in the senses].

The senses must give us the material and the matter, and this material is worked on by the mind. But with respect to the form of the concepts, it is intellectual. The first source of cognition thus lies in the material which the senses offer. The second source of cognition lies in the spontaneity of the mind. If the human only has the material, then he can always make ever new ideas. E.g. once he already has the concept of colour, he can form new ideas through the mixing of colours which have never at all existed in nature. But you cannot imagine new senses at all, because we lack the material for it. The senses thus are a necessary principle of cognition.

But we also have a principle of cognition through concepts which receives nothing at all from the senses; that is, we have knowledge of objects to the extent we are not at all influenced by the senses, and those are *intellectual* concepts. There are thus sensory and intellectual concepts. We could therefore say that there is nothing in the mind concerning matter which was not in the senses; but concerning the form there is know-ledge which is intellectual, which is not an object of the senses at all. E.g. in ethics the sensory knowledge forms the base *a posteriori*; but the mind also has base concepts. Only this must be adduced: that even the concepts of the mind, al-though they are not derived from the senses, originate though with the occasion of experience; e.g. nobody would have the concept of cause and effect if they had not experienced causes through experience. No human would have the concept of vir-tue if they were always among utter scoundrels. Accordingly the senses indeed constitute in this respect the base of all knowledge, although not all knowledge has its origin from them. — Although they are not the *principium essendi* [the principle of being], they are though a *conditio sine qua non* [a required condition].

But how do they arrive in the mind? They need not be as-sumed to be uncreated and unborn; for that puts an end to all investigation, and is very unphilosophical. If they are innate, then they are revelations. Crusius had a head full of such raptures, and he was lucky that he could think of such things. The concepts, however, originated through the mind according to its nature on the occasion of experience; for the mind forms on the occasion of experience and the senses concepts which are derived not from the senses, but rather from reflection over the senses. Locke went very much astray here in that he believed he could deduce all his concepts through experience; since he deduced them though from the reflection which was applied to the objects of the senses. Thus with respect to the material everything originates from the senses; with respect to the form from the mind, but the form is not innate to the mind, instead arising through reflection on the occasion of experience. We exercise this act of reflection whenever we have impressions of the senses. Through habit this reflection becomes familiar for us so that we do not notice that we are reflecting; and then we believe that it lies in the sensory view.

Now we want to see how far the concepts depend on reflection. We can namely have knowledge of objects of which we have no experience at all through the senses. Thus someone born blind can have the knowledge of light, just like a sighted person, which his mind offers to him; only that he does not have the experience, and over that we also cannot speak; for everyone has their own experience with the word *light*. We can thus separate the impressions from the judgements. The knowledge of the senses through the mind is something different from the knowledge through impressions. If we now consider the reflections over the experience to be impressions, then we commit an error of discrimination. The objects of the senses induce us to judgements. These judgements are experiences to the extent they are true; but if they are temporary judgements, then they are an appearance. The appearance precedes the experience; for it is a temporary judgement by the mind over the objects of the senses. The appearance is not true and also not false; for it is the cause for a judgement from experience. The appearance must thus be distinguished from the phenomenon. The phenomenon lies in the senses; the appearance is, however, only the cause of judging from the phenomenon. The perception is based both on the appearance and on the actual objects of experience; e.g. that the sun rises and it goes down signifies an appearance. From the appearance of the objects arises an illusion, and also a deception of the senses. Illusion is yet no deception of the senses; it is a temporary judgement that contradicts straightaway what follows. We very much love such illusions; e.g. we are not deceived by a peep box; for we know that it is not so; we are, however, moved to a judgement which is straightaway disproved by the mind. Illusions are different from the deception of the senses; with illusions I discover the deception. Because the objects of the senses cause us to make judgements, the errors are falsely ascribed to the senses, since they are actually to be attributed to the reflection over the senses. Accordingly we will note the sentence: *Sensus non fallunt* [they do not deceive the senses]. This does not happen because they judge correctly, but rather because they do not judge at all, but in the senses lie the appearance. They lead to judgements, although they do not deceive. The sentence gives us occasion to examine the grounds for the judgements, and to discover the deception through its solution. This sentence gives us cause thus to get behind the reason for errors. General concepts do not arise through the senses, but rather through the mind.

Only individual judgements arise through the senses; we thus do not receive through it the concept of cause and effect, not even the concept of lacking; for negation cannot influence the senses, and I cannot say that I have seen that nobody is in the room; for I cannot see the nothing.

Since we have considered, with sensoriality, the ideas of the senses themselves, which can also be called the means of experience; and also meaning, to the extent we arrive at ideas and knowledge, so far as we are influenced by the objects (knowledge is only possible to the extent the objects have an influence on our senses); we now want to consider the *emulated cognition of the senses*, which is also called quite properly the *forming power*; which is a capability of making knowledge from ourselves, but which therefore has the form in itself according to which the objects would influence our senses. This capablity of forming thus belongs really to sensoriality; it brings forth ideas either of the *present* time, or ideas of *past* times, or even ideas of *future* times. Therefore the capability of forming consist of:

1. the capability of *illustration*, which is ideas of the *present* time; *facultas formandi*;
2. the capability of *replication*, which is ideas of *past* times; *facultas imaginandi*;
3. the capability of *foreknowledge*, which is ideas of *future* times; *facultas praevidendi*.

My disposition is at any time busy with forming the image of the diversity while going through it. E.g. when I see a city, the disposition forms from the objects which it has before itself a picture while it runs through the diversity. Hence when a person enters a room which is cluttered with pictures and decorations, they cannot make a picture of it in that their disposition cannot run through the diversity. They do not know from which end it should begin to portray the objects. Thus it is reported of when a stranger arrives at St Peter's in Rome that he is quite shocked because of the diversity of the splendour. The cause is that his soul cannot go through the diversity in order to portray it. This illustrative capability is the forming capability of *contemplation*. The disposition must draw many observations in order to portray an object; as it portrays the object differently from each side. E.g. so a city looks differently in the morning than in the evening. There are thus many phenomena of a thing according to the various sides and viewpoints. From all these phenomena the disposition, as it brings them all together, must make an illustration.

The *second* capability is the capability of *replication* according to which my disposition draws the ideas of the senses from previous times, and connects them with the ideas of the present. I reproduce the ideas of the past by association, according to which one idea draws out the other because they were accompanied by them. This is the capability of imagination. It is otherwise falsely named the capability of fantasy, but that is of an entirely different sort; for it is something else entirely when I imagine a palace which I have seen previously, and when I make *new* pictures. The last is the capability of fantasy of which hereafter a report will be made.

The *third* capability is the capability of foreknowledge. Although the future makes no impression in me and thus no image, but rather only the present does; you can make an image of the future beforehand though, and imagine something beforehand. E.g. you imagine the form in which you will be if you want to hold a talk. But how is a foreknowledge of the future possible? The present phenomenon has ideas of the past and the following time. In my ideas, however, there is a series of consequent ideas where the ideas of the past relate to the present thus like the ideas of the present relate to the future. Just as the present state follows the past, the future follows on from the present. This happens according to the laws of imagination.

This difference of the forming power concerns time. There is, however, still another difference according to which we yet receive two capabilities of the forming power. These capabilities are the *capability of fantasy* and the *capability of analogues*. The capability of *fantasy* is the capability of bringing forth images from outside oneself, independently of the reality of the objects, where the images are not borrowed from experience. E.g. a master builder feigns to build a house which he has not yet seen. This capability is called the capability of *fantasy*, and must not be confused with that of imagination. The power of fantasy is a sensory power of fiction, although we also have a mental power of fiction.

The *capability of analogues* is the capability of characterisation. Characterisation is the analogue of the other. An analogue is a capability of bringing forth the image of the other thing. Thus words are analogues of things in order to conceive the ideas of the thing. Because it thus introduces images it belongs to sensoriality, although the images do not arrive through the influence of objects, but rather from ourselves; but according to form it belongs to sensoriality.

Finally you can add yet a *capability of development*. We do not only have a capability, but also an urge to develop and complete everything. Thus as things, stories, comedies or the like seem to be deficient to us; we are incessantly troubled to finish them; you are irritated that the thing is not whole. This assumes a capability of making an idea of the whole, and of comparing the objects with the idea of the whole.

All these acts of the forming power could happen both *voluntarily* and *involuntarily*. In so far as they happen *involuntarily* they belong entirely to sensoriality; but in so far as they happen *voluntarily* they belong to the higher means of cognition. *Memory* is thus a capability of voluntarily imagination or replication; thus there is no essential difference between memory and the capability of replication. It is also thus with other forming capabilities. Hypochondriac persons have involuntary fantasies. The voluntary capability of fantasy is the capability of poetry.

We must note yet in somewhat more detail of the capability of analogues or *Facultate characteristica* [faculty of characterising]: an idea which serves as the capability of reproduction by association is a *Symbolum* [symbol]. Most symbolic ideas happen with the cognition of God. These are altogether *per analogiam* [by analogy], i.e. through an agreement of the conditions; e.g. the sun was a symbol with the ancient peoples, an idea of divine perfection in that it, present everywhere in the great world construction, shares much (light and warmth) without receiving. Thus the human body can serve for the symbol of a republic in which all the components make up a whole. A cognition of the mind which is indirectly intellectual and is perceived through the mind, but is brought forth by an analogy of sensory knowledge, is a symbolic cognition, that of logical cognition, just as the intuitive is contrasted to the discursive. The cognition of the mind is logical when it is indirectly intellectual, and is brought forth by an analogy of sensory knowledge, but is perceived through the mind. The symbolum is only a means of conveying the intellection; it serves only the direct cognition of the mind; with time, however, it must fall away. The knowledge of all oriental nations is symbolic. Where experience is thus not directly allowed us, we must make do *per analogiam* with symbolic cognition. We can also say that the cognition is symbolic where the object is perceived in signs; but with discursive cognition the signs are not symbola in that I do not perceive the object in the signs, but rather the signs only bring forth the idea of the object. E.g. the word table is not a symbol, but rather just a capability of bringing forth the idea of the mind through association.

Of the higher capabilities of cognition

After we have dealt with the *lower* capabilities of cognition or with the ideas which we have of the objects to the extent we are influenced by them (thus reacted sufferingly to), we now come to the *higher* capabilities of cognition, or to the ideas which we have through voluntary exercise where we are the originator of the ideas.

General considerations over this:

The mind is not a means of regulation alone, but rather its principle is also that all our knowledge and objects must stand under one law. All phenomena stand under one law; for all objects to the extent they *appear*, they appear in relationship to time and space. But to the extent they are *thought*, they must stand under one law; for otherwise they cannot be thought. Thus what makes a law impossible is adverse to the mind.

The maxim of the mind is that everything which happens happens according to laws, and all knowledge is under one law. The more knowledge that can be derived from one *principio a priori*, the more unity the law has. But how do the pure mental concepts arrive in the head? We have knowledge of objects of contemplation by virtue of the forming power which is between the mind and sensoriality. When this forming power is *in abstracto*, it is the mind. These conditions and actions of forming power, taken *in abstracto*, are pure concepts of the mind and categories of the mind. E.g. the pure mental concept of substance and accident comes in the following way from the forming power: the forming power must be underlain by something constant, instead of the diversity changing; for if nothing were at the foundation of the forming power, then they could also change nothing. The constant now is the pure concept of substance, and diversity of accident. All the highest principles of mind are *a priori* general laws which express the conditions of the forming power in all phenomena with which we can determine how the phenomena are connected to one another; for that which makes knowledge possible was the condition of it, the same is also the condition of the things. We have principles *a priori* which are founded on the condition of contemplation; e.g. all axioms of geometry. Likewise we have also established principles of thinking *a priori*. What the necessary condition of thinking is depends on the objective, and what a necessary condition of contemplation is depends on the things too. The objects must be in agreement with the conditions under which they can be recognised; that is the nature of the human mind. The mind is thus *a priori* the means of reflecting over objects. The mind does not pass over the boundaries of the objects of the senses, but does go *up to the boundary*; that is God and the future world.

The *higher* capabilities of cognition are called thus because in them spontaneity is seen, since in the lower capabilities of cognition there was passivity. The higher means of cognition are also called the mind, in general minds. In this meaning the mind is the capability of concepts, or also the capability of judgements, but also the capability of laws. All three of these definitions are the same; for a concept is a knowledge which can serve for a predicate in a possible judgement. A concept is, however, an idea of comparison with the general feature, and a concept is a general feature. A judgement is, however, also always a law; for a law gives the relationship of the specific to the general. E.g. Cicero is learned; there the predicate *learned* serves for assessment of the actions of Cicero; thus it serves for a law. Accordingly the three definitions lead to one. We can also say the mind is the capability of general knowledge. General knowledge as ideas are concepts, and general knowledge as comparison of ideas are judgements; each general judgement is thus a law.

Sensoriality is a capability of contemplation. Parallel to sensoriality is the mind as the capability of concepts. Sensoriality has original forms; the mind, however, is a capability of laws; through that it distinguishes itself from sensoriality which only exists in forms. The senses are a capability of perception, but the mind of reflection. When you say the mind is a capability of distinct knowledge, then this is falsely defined; for sensoriality rests in the end on consciousness. Consciousness is, however, necessary for all knowledge and ideas; accordingly sensory knowledge can also be clear. But because consciousness is a *conditio sine qua non* [necessary condition] of knowledge, it is counted amongst the higher capabilities of cognition. Clarity is, however, not a necessary condition of mental knowledge in that there can also be a clarity of contemplation. The clarity of concepts is, however, mental clarity. All in if we define the mind negatively, in contrast with sensoriality, then the mind is a capability of recognising things independently of the way they appear to us. It seems indeed that if I define the mind as a capability of recognising things as they are, such a definition is not negative; only if I consider it in contrast to sensoriality do I not know though (if namely sensoriality recognises things as they appear, but the mind as they are) *how* the mind recognises them; I know only so much *that it does not recognise them as they appear*. This definition has its uses in that it is general, and is directed not only to the human mind, but rather to the mind overall.

But how can I recognise things as they are? Either through contemplation or concepts. The human mind is only a capability of recognising things as they are, through concepts and reflection, thus is merely discursive. All our knowledge is only logical and discursive, but not ostensive and intuitive. We can, however, think of a mind which recognises the things as they are, but through contemplation. Such a mind is intuitive. *There can be such a mind, only the human mind is not one.* This definition gives cause for the *mystical idea of the mind*. When we think namely of the human mind as a capability of recognising things as they are through contemplation, then it is *a mystical mind*; e.g. if we believe that in the soul a capability of intellectual contemplation lies, then such a thing is mystical mind. We have a capability of recognising things as they are, but not through contemplation, rather through concepts. If these concepts are pure concepts of mind, then they are transcendental. But when they apply to phenomena, they are empirical concepts, and the use of the mind is an empirical use.

Just as we have now weighed the mind, so too is it opposed to sensoriality and is called the higher capabilities of cognition. This mind taken in general, and the higher capabilities of cognition are threefold: *mind, power of judgement*, and *reason*. Here the mind is taken strictly where it is a species of the general significance of the mind and signifies the higher capabilities of cognition. These higher capabilities of cognition consist thus of:

1. a general judgement;

2.   a subsumption under this judgement; and

3.   the conclusion.

The principle of general judgement or laws is the *mind* taken strictly. The principle of subsumption under this law is the *power of judgement*, and the principium a priori of the law is *reason*. What cannot be subsumed under any empirical judgement is a judgement a priori. The capability of judgement which cannot be subsumed under any empirical judgement is reason. You can also say reason is the capability of laws a priori, or of concepts a priori.

In all parts, even in empirical knowledge, I need my mind, and that is the empirical use of mind. But we can also have a use of the mind a priori, and this is reason. E.g. everything accidental has a cause; here is the use of the mind a priori; for no experience teaches me that. Mind and reason are thus only differentiated in view of the empirical and pure use. Only we also have an intermediate capability between the two, namely subsuming under a general judgement and under a general law; and that is the power of judgement. First of all I ask: is the general law a priori or a posteriori? And then: whether the case belongs under the law? E.g. that every individual thinks is a law a priori. Now I see whether the soul of the human belongs under this law and can be subsumed under it. This capability of subsuming under laws is so separate from other capabilities that humans can indeed have a capability of the general law; but entirely without having this capability of subsuming under the law, and employing the law *in concreto* [in a particular case].

Mind is the capability of recognising from the general the particular; the power of judgement of recognising from the particular the general; and the reason to recognise the general *a priori*, and to collect laws from the various phenomena. The particular is given here from which you make a general law. But the power of judgement is the reverse; there a general law is given from which the particular must be determined. Thus in order to know whether the particular belongs under the general law, the power of judgement is needed. This has the special feature inherent to it *that it cannot be learned through instruction*, but rather you must obtain skill at it through practice. The mind may be instructed, but not the power of judgement. Reason is the capability of recognising general laws *a priori* entirely abstracted from experience. E.g. everything accidental must have a first cause; experience does not teach this.

The extents of the mind rest on two parts, on the capability of concepts, and on the relation of general concepts to particular cases. The more the judgement has a relation to the particular cases, the more spread out and extensively clearer the mind is; and the more the mind is connected with contemplations, the more spread out and brighter it is. Anyone who can accordingly put to good use the general laws in examples, analogies, and special cases of common life has an expanded mind. The mind is thus instructed in a twofold way:

a) that you accustom it to general laws, or use *in abstracto* [in the abstract], and

b) that you use these general laws in experience, or use *in concreto*.

Here you do not have to believe that the latter is all one with the power of judgement; for the power of judgment is only a capability of knowing whether a given case belongs under the law; which is different from the mind *in concreto* which is used in the cases of experience. The mind *in concreto* is only a capability of remembering the general law; you cannot differentiate by that alone whether the given case falls under the general law. The power of judgement, however, is a capability of differentiation.

The use of reason is also twofold:

a) a pure, and

b) an empirical use.

The pure use of reason is that which applies to objects which are not objects of the senses at all. The empirical use is when I recognised something *a priori* which is confirmed *a posteriori*; e.g. in experimental physics. A pure use of reason is that where the rule is not confirmed by experience. But where the rule is itself taken from experience, then it is not a use of reason.

We can still differentiate all three of these capabilities which constitute the higher capabilities of cognition into *healthy* and *learned* capabilities. Thus we have then a healthy mind, a healthy power of judgement, and a healthy reason;

but also a speculative mind, a speculative power of judgement and reason. The healthy use of these capabilities shows itself *in concreto* in the cases where experience can make the argument from the correctness of this power of cognition. If I use my mind, my power of judgement, and reason thus that through the experience it can be made out that it is true, then I have a healthy mind, a healthy power of judgement and reason. If I do not go any further with my powers of cognition than as far as it can confirm the experience, then that is the healthy use of the powers of cognition. Speculative use of the mind and of reason is to the extent they have a capability of using the law without experience. Speculative power of judgement is where the grounds for the correct use are not in experience, but rather lie in general grounds.

With respect to knowledge, *temperament* and *genius* are distinguished. — Temperament is a tendency for learning, but genius for finding knowledge which cannot be learned at all. The *head* is the talent of knowledge. Heads are distinguished, with respect to skill, into fine and dull; with respect to the objects into mathematical and philosophical heads. Anthropology deals with this in detail.

Before we pass over to the capability of pleasure and displeasure, we must still (as a transition of the upper capabilities of cognition to the capability of differentiation of the objects according to feeling, pleasure and displeasure) deal with the *capability of comparing*, and of recognising objects in comparison. The forming capability, or the capability of cognition, is a capability of producing ideas. Now we also have yet a capability of comparing ideas, and that is *wit* and *acumen*. Wit (*ingenium*) is the capability of comparing objects according to differences. The capability of agreement or sameness lies at the base of our general concepts. In each judgement I recognise that something either belongs under the general concept or not; this is *ingenium*. E.g. whether foxes belong under the general concepts of dogs. You can thus seek comparison and agreement in all of nature. Only when I have a negative judgement, when I find that it does not belong to the general concept, but rather is different from it, then it is *acumen*. The expressions of acumen are those whereby we protect our knowledge from errors, and thus purify them, when we say what the things are not. By *ingenium* we expand our knowledge, *ingenium* is thus the first thing. At first I make all sorts of comparisons, but then comes *acumen*, and distinguishes one from the other. So at first humans will have considered according to inherent nature everything hard to be stone, but after that they will have gradually distinguished one from another. You do not really know to what this capability can actually be attributed, whether to the lower or higher capabilities of cognition. In general it is the higher capabilities of cognition applied to the lower. It thus belongs probably to the higher capabilities of cognition.

Of the capability of pleasure and displeasure

The second capability of the soul is the capability of distinguishing things according to the feelings of pleasure and displeasure, or of liking and disliking. The capability of pleasure and displeasure is not a capability of cognition, but rather is entirely different from that. The determinations of things in respect to which we show pleasure and displeasure are not determinations which merely befit the objects, but rather refer to the composition of the subject. Through the capability of cognition I cannot have different ideas of the things than according to the determination which would be made of them, even if they were not imagined at all; e.g. I would recognise the round figure by a circle without a circle being imagined. But the determinations of good and evil, of beautiful and ugly, of pleasant and unpleasant, are determinations which cannot be perceived in the things at all if they are not recognised by imagination. Therefore such determinations, which cannot be recognised in the things without imagination, cannot belong to the capability of cognition because the latter, even without idea of the things, can recognise the determinations belonging to them; but rather there must be a *special* capability in us of perceiving such in them. It is thus not determinations which refer in the circumstances to our capability of cognition, but rather to a quite different capability whose condition is indeed certainly the capability of cognition, for without it I cannot have any pleasure or displeasure from objects; but it is a special capability which is distinguished from the capability of cognition. When I talk of objects to the extent they are beautiful or ugly, pleasant or unpleasant, I do not know the object in itself, just as it is, but rather as it affects me. When Euclid talks of the circle, he does not describe it to the extent it is beautiful, but rather as it is in itself. But in order to recognise something as beautiful etc., a special capability exists in us, but not in the object. If we take away from all rational beings the capability of pleasure and displeasure, and also increase their capability of cognition just as much, then they would recognise all objects without being stirred by them; it would be all the same to them; for the capability of being influenced by objects would be lacking. All pleasure and displeasure assumes knowledge of objects, either a knowledge of sensation, or of contemplation, or of the concepts, and so as they say: *ignota nulla cupido* [no unknown desire], so you could also say: *ignoti nulla complacentia* [no unknown complacency]. Only it is not the cognition in which the pleasure is found, but rather *the feeling* for which the cognition is the condition.

All predicates of the things which express the pleasure and displeasure are not predicates which approach the objects in and of themselves, or predicates which stand in relationship to our power of cognition, but rather they are predicates of the capability in us of being influenced by the things. It has been said that this capability was a cognition of the perfection and imperfection of objects, only perfection is not the feeling of the beautiful and pleasant, but rather perfection is the completeness of the object. Now it is certainly true that all completeness pleases, and we have a capability of applying the idea of completeness to everything, and of forming everything completely; only to recognise the completeness, i.e. the perfection of the object, is not a recognition of pleasure, but rather it still questions whether they are connected in certain cases to pleasure and displeasure. Assuming that the object is an object of pleasure; thus the perfection also pleases, and then the completeness is also not always necessary for pleasure. With pleasure and displeasure it is not about the object, but rather *how* the object influences the disposition. Pleasure and displeasure are capabilities whereby objects are differentiated, not by something found in themselves, but rather by how the idea of them makes an impression on our subject, and how our feeling is stirred by them.

But what is a *feeling*? That is something difficult to define. We feel ourselves. The ideas can be twofold: ideas of the object and of the subject. Our ideas can be compared, either with the objects, or with the entire life of the subject. The subjective idea of the entire life power of receiving or excluding the objects is the relationship of liking or disliking. Thus the feeling is not the relationship of the objects to the idea, but rather to the entire power of the disposition to either intimately receive or exclude them. The receiving is the feeling of pleasure and the excluding of displeasure. *The beautiful is thus not the relationship of cognition to the object, but rather to the subject.* Nothing more can be said about this here. Accordingly we have two perfections: *logical* and *aesthetic*. The first perfection is that when my cognition agrees with the object, and the second perfection is that when my cognition agrees with the subject.

We have an inner principle of acting from ideas, and that is life. If now an idea harmonises with the entire power of the disposition, with the principle of life, then this is *pleasure*. But when the idea is of the sort that resists the principle of life, then this relationship of resistance is in us *displeasure*. The objects are accordingly beautiful, ugly, etc. not in and of themselves, but rather in respect to the living being. *But what only takes place in reference to the living being must have its grounds in the living being*; accordingly there must be a *capability* in the living being of perceiving such characteristics in the objects. Thus pleasure and displeasure are a capability of agreement or of resistance of the principle of life against certain ideas or impressions of objects.

Life is the inner principle of self-activation. Living beings which act according to this inner principle must also act according to ideas. Now there can be both a furtherance and a hindrance to life. The feeling of the furtherance of life is pleasure, and the feeling of the hindrance to life is displeasure. Pleasure is thus a grounds of activity, and displeasure a hindrance to activity. Pleasure exists thus in desire; displeasure by contrast in loathing. — Now we see what pleasure and displeasure have in order to link with the thinking being.

Only active beings can have pleasure and displeasure. Subjects who are then acting according to ideas have pleasure and displeasure. Thus a creature which is not acting according to ideas has no capability for pleasure and displeasure.

Life is threefold:

1. the *animal,*
2. the *human,* and
3. the *spiritual* life.

There are thus three sorts of pleasure. The *animal pleasure* consists of the feelings of the private senses. The *human pleasure* is the feelings according to the general sense, by means of the sensory power of judgement; it is a something in between and is known through the idea from sensoriality. The *spiritual pleasure* is idealistic, and is known from pure concepts of the mind. Pleasure or displeasure, liking or disliking is either objective or subjective. If the basis of the liking or disliking of the object agrees with the specific subject, then this is subjective liking or disliking. This originates from the senses. Each special sense is a basis for subjective liking. Thus what pleases or displeases according to the private grounds of the sense of a subject is the subjective liking or disliking. The liking from private grounds of the sense of a subject is *enjoyment,* and the object is pleasant. The disliking from private grounds of the sense of a subject is *discontentment* or *pain,* and the object is unpleasant. But if I say that something is pleasant or unpleasant, then that expresses only a subjective liking or disliking from privately valid grounds of liking or disliking. Because a certain object always seems pleasant or unpleasant, it does not follow that it must seem so to everybody. You cannot therefore argue about it. The *objective* liking or disliking consists of the pleasure and displeasure in the object, not in the relationship to special conditions of the subject; but rather, independently from the special conditions of the subject, to the general judgement which has a general validity and applies to everybody. Thus that which is a general basis for the generally valid liking or disliking is an *objective* liking or disliking. This objective liking or disliking is twofold: something is liked or disliked *either* according to the general sensoriality, *or* according to the general power of cognition. What then is liked from the agreement with the general sense is *beautiful*; and if it is disliked from the same basis it is *ugly*. What is liked from the agreement with the general power of cognition is *good*; and if it is disliked from the same basis, then it is *evil*.

That which the minds of humans agree on is the *general* sense. But how can a human make a judgement according to the general sense when he is though considering the object according to his private sense? The community among humans constitutes a general sense. From the contact with humans a general sense arises which applies to everybody. Thus anyone who does not enter into any community will have no general sense. — The beautiful and the ugly can only be distinguished by humans to the extent that they are in the community. Thus anyone to whom something is pleasing according to a communal and commonly applicable sense has *taste*. Taste is therefore a capability of judgement through liking or disliking, according to the communal and generally applicable sense. But taste is always only ever a judgement by relationship of the mind and hence this capability is a capability of pleasure and displeasure.

The objective liking or disliking, or judging of objects according to generally applicable grounds of the power of cognition, is the higher capability of pleasure and displeasure. That is the capability of judging from knowledge of the mind according to generally applicable principles whether the object pleases or displeases. If something is an object of intellectual pleasure, then it is good; if an object of intellectual displeasure, then it is evil. Good is what anyone must by necessity like. The beautiful, however, does not please everyone by necessity, but rather the agreement with the judgement is accidental. But the agreement with the judgement of liking or disliking through the mind, according to whether the object is either good or evil, is by necessity. But how can the good please, when it awakens no delight? If virtue were pleasant, then everyone would be virtuous; but now each wishes only, if it were possible, to be virtuous all of a sudden. He sees that it is good; only it does not please him. *Freedom* is the highest degree of activity and of life. Animal life has no spontaneity. If I now feel that something agrees with the highest degree of freedom, thus agrees with the intellectual life, then it pleases me. This pleasure is intellectual pleasure. You have a pleasure in it without it delighting. Such intellectual pleasure is only in *ethics*. From where, however, has ethics such pleasure? All morality is the harmonisation of freedom with itself. For example, someone who lies is not in agreement with his freedom because he is bound by the lie. *But whatever is in agreement with freedom agrees with the entire life. But whatever agrees with the entire life pleases*. This is though only a reflective pleasure; we find no delight here, but rather approve it through reflection. Virtue thus has no delight, but applause for it; for the human feels his spiritual/intellectual life and the highest degree of his freedom.

Now we can make the following division. Something is an object of pleasure in the perception; or an object of pleasure in the contemplation; or the sensory general power of judgement, i.e. an object of pleasure according to the concepts of the mind. If something pleases in the perception, then it *delights*, and the object is pleasant. That which is an object of contemplation or of the sensory power of judgement *pleases*, and the object is beautiful. That which is an object of pleasure according to the concepts of the mind is *approved of*, and the object is good. In order to distinguish the pleasant and unpleasant, we need feeling; to distinguish the beautiful and the ugly, we need taste; to distinguish good and evil, we need reason. For the investigation of the pleasant and unpleasant, we have no common standard, because it is with respect to the private perception of the subject. Hence you cannot get involved in any argument over the pleasant or unpleasant; for an argument is an endeavour to bring the other to agreement with one's judgement. But because each here has his private perception, neither can be forced to accept the other perception. With the beautiful, however, it is different. There it is not the beautiful which pleases one, but rather what everyone applauds; regardless of whether it is also equally liked through the mind, but by a general sense. For the investigation of the beautiful and the ugly, we thus have a general standard; this is the communal sense. This communal sense comes into being thus: each private perception is not though an entirely special perception, but rather the private perception of the one must agree with the private perception of the others, and by this agreement we arrive at a general rule. This is the communal sense or *taste*. Whatever then agrees is beautiful. This can now indeed probably not please one private sense, but it pleases according to the general rule. Whomever it does not please, those whose private sense does not agree with the general rule, have no taste. Taste is thus the power of judgement of the senses whereby that is recognised which agrees with the senses of others; it is thus a pleasure and displeasure in communion with others. The general agreement of the sensoriality is what constitutes with taste the grounds for liking. For example, a house is beautiful, not because it delights through contemplation (for then the eatery would perhaps delight some better); but rather because it is an object of common liking; because thousands can have a delight in one and the same object. It is thus also the case with music. Sight and hearing are accordingly senses of taste and communal. Smell, however, and taste are only private senses of perception. Pleasant is that which agrees with the private senses; but beautiful is that which agrees with the communal senses. There can be arguments over the beautiful, because many people's agreement gives a judgement which can be placed against an individual judgement. Taste has its rule; for every general agreement in a feature is the foundation of the rule. These rules are not *a priori*, and not in and of themselves, but rather they are empirical, and the sensoriality must be recognised *a posteriori*. Accordingly you can probably argue over the rule *a posteriori*, but not dispute it. For disputing means opposing the grounds of the other from principles of reason. It is wrong if you say: the person has a quite special taste; for if he chooses what displeases everyone else, he has no taste, because taste must be judged according to the communal sense. If a person were entirely alone on an island, then he would not choose according to taste, but according to appetite. Thus only in the society of others does he have taste. Taste brings forth nothing new, but rather it merely presents that which is brought forth so that it pleases all.

You could also say that a few rules of taste would be *a priori*; but not directly *a priori*, but rather comparatively, so that these rules base themselves *a priori* again on general rules of experience. For example, the order, the symmetry, the harmony in music are rules where I recognise and understand *a priori* that they please everyone, but which base themselves again on general rules *a posteriori*. We could also claim a necessary taste; for example, everyone has a taste for Homer, Cicero, Virgil, etc.

The good is an object of the mind and is judged through the mind. We call an object *in itself* good, and not in relation. If I say the thing is *good*, then I am saying this without reference to other objects. But if I say the thing is *beautiful*, then I only say how I feel about it, and how it appears to me. The good must thus also please such beings who have no such sensoriality as we do; which, however, is not how things stand with the pleasant and the beautiful. Something is good either directly or indirectly. Something is good *indirectly* if it coincides with something else as a means to an end. *Directly* good is that which pleases generally and necessarily in and of itself.

To summarise everything which is to be said about pleasure and displeasure; it is thus noted that all pleasure and displeasure is either sensory or intellectual. The lower capability, or the sensory pleasure and displeasure, rests on the picturing of the object through sensoriality. The upper capability of pleasure and displeasure, or the intellectual pleasure and displeasure, rests on the picturing of the object by the mind. Sensory pleasure and displeasure is twofold; either it rests on the conditions of sensory perception, or on sensory contemplation. The pleasure is in relation to sensory perception to the extent it agrees with the state of the subject, to the extent the latter is changed by the object. It pleases sensually, but subjectively, and thence the object is pleasant. — The pleasure is in relation to sensory contemplation to the extent it merely agrees overall with the capability of sensoriality, i.e. it pleases sensually and objectively, and then the object is beautiful. On this thus rests the differences of the beautiful and the pleasant, the sensory enjoyments, and the enjoyments according to taste. When the object only agrees with the state of the subject, then it cannot please in general, but rather according to the private pleasure of the subject. But if the object agrees with the general laws of sensoriality overall, then it must also please generally. To the general laws of sensoriality belongs, for example, that perceived in the object are order, the idea of the whole, etc. What now applies in relation to a general judgement for anyone pleases objectively. But that which applies in relation to a private judgement pleases subjectively. Feeling is therefore not to be cultivated like taste, because feeling only applies to me, but taste is general. Intellectual pleasure is that which pleases generally, but not according to the general laws of sensoriality, but rather according to the general laws of understanding. The object of intellectual pleasure is good. The beautiful is indeed also an object which pleases in general, but according to general laws of sensoriality; the good pleases, however, according to the general laws of understanding. The good is independent of the way the object appears to the senes; it must be taken as it is in and of itself; for example, truthfulness.

An object is indifferent to the extent it is neither an object of pleasure nor of displeasure. Such objects are called *Adiaphora* [morally neutral values]. Adiaphora can be either aesthetic or logical; either according to the laws of sensoriality, or of understanding. *Adiaphora aesthetica* are those that are neither unpleasant nor pleasant, neither beautiful nor ugly. *Adiaphora logica* are those which are neither good nor evil. Some say there are no Adiaphora. There are certainly no *Adiaphora absoluta* where a thing is supposed to be in no circumstances good nor evil; only in specific cases are there the like though — e.g. whether I should give a poor person alms with the right or left hand, etc. But if you wanted to reckon among the Adiaphora an act which belongs under the law of morals, then this would be extremely harmful. Where there is a generally defined law, no Adiaphora apply; but where there is no general law defining something, then there can be Adiaphora.

Of the capability of desiring

The third capability of our soul is the capability of desiring. The capability of pleasure and displeasure was the relationship of the object to our feeling of the activity, either of the advancement or of the hindrance of life. But to the extent the capability of pleasure and displeasure is a capability of specific activities and actions which are in accordance with them, to that extent it is a *desire*. Desire *is thus a pleasure to the extent it is a grounds for the activity of determining certain ideas of the object*. If the idea is a basis for committing to the object, then we *desire* the object. The dislike of an object, to the extent it can be the cause of the idea, is *loathing*. The pleasure of the activity to bring forth the idea is twofold: either we decide on this activity as it were problematically ˙without appreciating whether it is appropriate to the bringing forth of the idea; or we decide on the idea to the extent we have appreciated its capability for bringing forth the idea. The first is a passive desire or a wish.

But there are yet two types of activity: the one is mechanical, and is brought forth by an alien power; the other is animal or practical. Here the force is determined from the inner principle. The capability of acting according to pleasure or displeasure is the practically active capability of desire. The capability of desire shall thus be active and consist in action. Only our capability of desire goes still further; we desire without also being active, without acting; that is a passive desire or yearning, where you desire something without being able to obtain it. The active desire, however, or the capability to do and to leave according to the pleasure or displeasure in the object, to the extent it is a cause of the active power to bring it forth, is the *free arbitrariness (arbitrium liberum)*. This desire is active and powerful, and has the force to achieve the desired. With each *arbitrio* are *causae impulsivae* [impulsive causes]. — *Causae impulsivae* are ideas of the object according to pleasure and displeasure, to the extent they are the causes of the determination of our power. Each *actus arbitrii* [arbitrary act] has *causam impulsivam*. — The *Causae impulsivae* are either sensitive or intellectual. The sensitive ones are *stimuli* or *causes of movement, drives*. The intellectual ones are *motives* or *grounds for movement*. The first are for the senses, the others for the mind. If the *Causae impulsivae* are ideas of pleasure or displeasure which depend on the way we are influenced by the objects, then that is *stimuli*. But when the *Causae impulsivae* are ideas of liking and

---

*   [Tr.: problematic in logic means only affirming the *possibility* that a predicate be actualised.]

34

disliking which then depend on the way we recognise the objects through concepts, through the mind, then that is motives. *Stimuli* are causes which impel the arbitrary will to the extent the object influences our senses. This driving power of the arbitrary will can either necessitate or it can also just simply impel. The stimuli thus have either *vim necessitantem* [necessitating energy] or *vim impellentem* [impulsive energy]. With all irrational animals the stimuli have *vim necessitantem*; but with humans the stimuli do not have *vim necessitantem*, but rather only *impellentem*. Therefore the *arbitrium humanum* [human judgement] is not *brutum* [irrational], but rather *liberum* [free]. This is the *arbitrium liberum* to the extent it is defined psychologically or practically. Only the same arbitrium which is not necessitated or impelled by any stimulus at all, but rather is determined through motives, through grounds for movement of the mind, is the *liberum arbitrium intellectuale* or *transcendentale*. The *arbitrium sensitivum* [sensitive judgement] can probably be *liberum*, but not the *brutum*. The *arbitrium sensitivum* is only influenced or impelled by the stimuli; but the *brutum* is necessitated. Humans thus have a free arbitrary will, and all that which originates from their arbitrary will originates from a *free* arbitrary will. All forms of torture cannot compel the human's free arbitrary will; he can endure them all and yet rely on his will. Only in a few cases does he have no free arbitrary will; for example, in the most tender childhood, or if he is insane, or in high sorrow, which is also a form of madness though. Humans feel thus a capability in themselves of not being forced to do anything by anything in the world. Indeed such things are more often difficult for other reasons; but it is yet possible they have the power for it. The *causae impulsivae* are, however, either *subjectivae*, or *objectivae*; according to the laws of sensoriality and according to the laws of the mind. The *Causae impulsivae subjectivae* are stimuli, and the *objectivae* are motives. — The *Necessitatio per motiva* [necessity through motives] is not contrary to freedom, but the *Necessitatio per stimulos* [necessity through stimulus] is entirely against the same. The free arbitrary will, to the extent it acts according to motives of the mind, is the freedom which in all intent is good. This is the *libertas absoluta* [absolute freedom], which is the moral freedom.

The *arbitrium humanum* is *liberum*, it may be *sensitivum* or *intellectuale*. What occurs on the side of sensibility is that the stimuli, to the extent they are in agreement with the vague suggestions, are called *instincts*; for example, you have an instinct for eating. Instincts are either appetites or aversions. For example, the little chick already has by nature an instinct of aversion for the hawk of which it fears as soon as it just sees something flying in the sky.

Concerning the degree of the sensory drives, we call them *affects* and *passions*. The affects work on the feelings, the passions on the desires. We are influenced by the affects, but we are carried away by the passions. Here it is all about the degree of freedom. The degree of the stimulus which is a hindrance to freedom is affect. In so far as the stimuli do not only hinder freedom, but rather also outweigh it, to that extent they are called passions.

Now we want to consider the stimuli in collision with freedom, or the sensoriality with the intellectuality, the sensory drives with the motives.

The mind presents motives to refrain from an action; the sensoriality by contrast presents stimuli to commit to it. This dispute ceases, however, either when the stimuli no longer urge (then the *facultas superior* wins, and the motives have the superiority); or when the mind no longer presents any motives at all; then the sensoriality gains the superiority. Now anyone who has power over the sensoriality and the mind so that the sensoriality does not become dominant has the *imperium in semetipsum* [superiority to himself].

The greatest freedom is reckoned with humans according to the degree of superiority of the hindrances. Our measure for determining the extent of freedom thus rests on the degree of superiority of the sensory drives. But there are beings who have no sensory drives at all; whose freedom we cannot estimate because they have no measure of this, for our measure of reckoning freedom is taken from the sensory drives.

Animals can be compelled *stricte per stimulos* [strictly through stimuli], but humans only *comparatively* so. This *coactio* [compulsion] can be either *externa* or *interna*. The *co-*

actio externa is the *coactio arbitrii liberi intellectualis* [compulsion of intellectual free will]. You can be forced through sensoriality to act against intellectuality; but you can also be forced through intellectuality to act against sensoriality. The more the human, by means of the higher arbitrary will, has power to suppress the lower arbitrary will, the freer he is. But the less he is able to force sensoriality by intellectuality; the less freedom he has. If you force yourself according to the rules of morality and suppress the lower arbitrary will by the higher arbitrary will, then that is *virtue.* — The *practical freedom*, or the freedom of the person, must be distinguished from the physical freedom, or from the freedom of condition. Personal freedom can remain even when the physical is missing, for example with Epictetus. This practical freedom rests on the *Independentia arbitrii a necessitatione per stimulos* [Independence of choice from necessity through stimuli]. That freedom which is, however, entirely independent from all stimuli is the transcendental freedom which is spoken of in the *Psychologia rationali**. Everything that occurs in nature occurs either according to physical-mechanical laws or according to the laws of free arbitrary will. In inanimate nature everything occurs according to mechanical laws, but in the animate according to the laws of free arbitrary will. What occurs according to the laws of arbitrary will occurs either *pathologically* or *practically*. Therefore something is pathologically necessary or possible according to the laws of sensory arbitrary will. — Something is practically necessary or possible according to the laws of free arbitrary will. Therefore the *Necessitatio* is either pathological or practical.

The *Necessitatio practica* can be of many sorts:

1. *Necessitatio problematica*, where the idea of necessity of the use of the means is recognised under the condition of the desired goal; for example in geometry.
2. *Necessitatio pragmatica*, where the idea of necessity of the use of the means is recognised in view of the general goal of any thinking being.

---

*   [Tr.: see 3 f. above.]

3. *Necessitatio moralis.* This is the necessity of the use of free arbitrary will, not for a goal, but rather because it is necessary in itself.

All sentences of practical necessitation are expressed through the imperative, that the action *shall* occur, i.e. it is good that the action occurs. There is thus no stimulus, and this practical necessitation is objective. An objective necessitation can also be subjective (the pathological is at all times subjective), if namely the mere cognition of the action, *that* it is good, moves my subject to exercise it; then it is a driving force. When the cognition of the mind has a power to move the subject to the action, *merely because* the action is good *in itself*, then this motive power is a driving force which we also call *moral feeling.* Moral feeling shall thus exist where a motive power arises through the motives of the mind. This driving force of the mood shall, however, not compel pathologically; and it also does not compel pathologically in that we see the good through the mind and not to the extent it influences our senses. We shall thus think a feeling which, however, does not compel, and this shall be the moral feeling. You should recognise the good through the mind, and yet have a feeling of it. This is certainly something which you cannot rightly understand, but which is also still argued over. I shall have a feeling of that which is not an object of feeling, but rather which I recognise objectively through the mind. Here there thus always lies a contradiction. For if we shall do good through feeling, then we are doing it because it is pleasant. But this cannot be, for the good cannot influence our senses at all. However, we call the liking of the good a feeling because we cannot express the driving power of the objectively practical necessitation any other way. It is a misfortune for the human race that the moral laws which then compel objectively do not also compel subjectively at the same time. If we were also at the same time subjectively compelled, then we would be just as free because this subjective necessitation arises from the objective. We are subjectively compelled by the condition that the action is objectively good. The moral necessity is at all times practical; but not every moral necessity is moral. If the motives enunciate the *bonum absolutum* [absolute good], then they are *motiva moralia* [moral

38

motives]. To the extent the motives enunciate the *bonum comparativa* [comparative good], to the extent they only say what in a qualified way is good, to that extent they are only *motiva pragmatica* [pragmatic motives]. Thus the *motiva moralia* must not be confused with the pragmatic.

The *indoles*, or the *disposition*, means the proportion of the principles and sources of our desires. *Indoles erecta* [uprght character] is the noble disposition where the higher means of desire reigns; *indoles abjecta* [low character] by contrast is the ignoble disposition where the lower means of desire, sensoriality, reigns.

Artes ingenuae and *liberales* [creative and liberal arts] are those which takes us from the desires of enjoyment to the desires of contemplation which frees the human from the servitude of the senses — for anyone who, for example, finds enjoyment in poetic things is already freed from the coarse sensoriality. The proportion amongst the sensory drives is *temperament*.

Of the commerce of the soul with the body

When we consider the soul of the human, we consider it not merely as intelligence, but rather as the soul of the human where it *stands in connection with the body*. Only it is not merely in connection, but rather also in *communion*; for we can also stand in connection with other bodies, for example with our children; but that is no communion. *The communion is the connection where the soul makes up a unity with the body; where the changes of the body are at the same time the changes of the soul and the changes of the soul are at the same time the changes of the body*. No changes occur in the disposition which do not correspond with the changes of the body. Furthermore not only does the change correspond, but rather also the *composition* of the disposition corresponds with the composition of the body. With respect to the correspondence of the changes, nothing can take place in the soul where the body should not come into play.

This occurs:

1. through thinking. The soul thinks nothing where the body should not be influenced through thinking. The body endures many attacks through thought, and is thereby very stressed.

The more the soul is active, the more the body is battered. The ideas of the soul correspond with something corporeal. These conditions of the body under which the thoughts can merely take place are called *ideas materiales* or material objects of the idea. Likewise we cannot immediately work out a large calculation in our heads (which indeed could be done with a small one), but instead must use numbers which correspond with our thoughts, and accompany the idea; for otherwise we could not think. In the brain there must thus be impressions of what has been thought; there must be something corporeal with thinking. The soul thus very much influences the brain through thinking. The brain certainly does not work out the thoughts, but rather it is just the board where the soul draws up its thoughts. Thus the brain is the condition of thought; for all our thinking applies to objects. The objects, however, are that which influences me. Accordingly thought applies to things which influence my body; thus my thought will be directed to the impressions of the brain which my body receives. These corporeal impressions are the *idea materiales*. From this it thus follows that the body is influenced along with the thought. We cannot continue in that investigation here.

2. *Wanting* influences our bodies still more than thought. The free arbitrary will moves the body as it likes; the arbitrary influence of desires on our bodies is entirely clear, of which the deliberate influence also is; but if our desires bring forth movements in the body contrary to our intention, movements though which have their natural origin (for example, if you are frightened by something and want to run away, and cannot or fall down out of fear); thus the intention was there to run; the falling down, however, must have followed here naturally out of fear. Thus the body is also very much influenced when the human falls into emotions and passions; for example, fury can often make one sick. This feeling also influences the body a lot; thus you can, for example, pale over a letter in which you receive sad news.

3. *External objects* also influence my senses. Through this the nerves are influenced, and through this affecting of the nerves the play of sensation occurs in the soul according to the capability of pleasure and displeasure, whereby the entire body

goes into motion according to that. On the other hand, the body again influences the disposition through its corporeal constitution. This corporeal constitution is the cause of the *indoles* and the temperament of the disposition. What the human has for a temperament depends a lot on the body; also the head, even the powers of disposition, seem to depend very much on the body. Thus you see in someone eyes already the cheerfulness of his mind and wit, and in another stupidity already radiates from his forehead. Much accordingly in respect to our desires and the means of pleasure and displeasure also rests on the body. On the other hand the composition and also the state of the disposition rests on the composition and state of the body. You can, for example, liven up the disposition through corporeal movement, and vice versa through movements of the disposition (e.g. in company) liven up the body again. We can thus get the better of the body through the disposition, and of the disposition through the body.

It is the question of what side is the most derived from, from the body or from the soul? Furthermore, would the soul, if it had come into a different body, have the same or a different composition and another state? Over this we can say *nothing*; for we are considering here the soul in communion with its body, and cannot thus know what the soul *without* this body, and the body *without* this soul would be. Many claim that all souls are all the same, and the differences of the diversity merely arise from the body. These are arriving at *materialism*. If we on the other hand place all power in the soul, then we arrive at *Stahlianism**. Stahl was a physician who claimed this. You cannot completely contradict this opinion, for all characteristics of the soul are already to be read in the demeanour and the features of the body; thus the soul must have placed its characteristics into the body. A few claim that it itself also makes its body.

To conclude the empirical psychology the question is to be posed of whether all the powers of the soul are united and can be derived *from a base power*, or whether various base powers are to be assumed in order thereby to explain all the

---

*   [Tr.: the teachings of Georg Ernst Stahl (1659–1734), a German alchemist, chemist, physician, and philosopher. He was a strong adherent of vitalism.]

actions of the soul. Wolff* assumes one base power and says the soul itself is a base power which represents the universe. It is already false when you say the soul is one base power. This turns out because the soul is defined falsely, as ontology teaches. Power is not what contains the base of the real idea in itself, but rather the *respectus* [looking back] of the substance to the accident, to the extent that the basis of the real ideas is contained in the same. *The power is thus not a special principle, but rather a respectus.* Anyone who thus says *anima est vis* [soul is the force] claims that the soul is not a special substance, but rather only a power, thus a phenomenon and contingent. In order to now answer and deal with the question of whether all powers of the soul can be derived from *one* base power, or whether several of those are to be assumed, we must certainly say that because the soul is a unity, which is made clear after this, and which already shows the ego, it is thus obvious that only *one* base power is in the soul, from which all alterations and determinations arise. Only that is a quite different question: whether we are capable of deriving all actions of the soul, and the various powers and capabilities of it, *from one base power?* This we are in no way capable of; for we cannot indeed derive effects, which are really different from each other, from *one* base power; e.g. the power of motion and the power of cognition cannot possibly be derived from *one* power; for the cause of the one power is different from that of the others. Since we now encounter in the human soul real determinations or accidents of a fundamental sort, every philosopher endeavours in vain to derive such from *one* base power. This is indeed the most important rule of the philosopher: that he endeavours as much as is possible to bring everything to *one* principle so that the principles of the sources of cognition are not augmented too much; but whether we also have in the human disposition cause to reduce various powers to *one* power does not follow from that. For example, memory is only an imagination of past things, thus no special base power. The imagination itself, however, we cannot derive further. Accordingly the cap-

---

* [Tr.: Christian Wolff (1679–1754) was a German philosopher and named by Kant as "the greatest of all dogmatic philosophers" in the second edition of *The Critique of Pure Reason.*]

ability of forming* is already a base power. Furthermore reason is thus only the mind *a priori*. We find therefore that we must assume various basic powers, and cannot explain from *one* all the phenomena of the soul; for who wants surely to endeavour to derive the mind from the senses? *Accordingly the capability of cognition, the capability of pleasure and displeasure, and the capability of desire are basic powers.* You endeavour in vain to derive all powers of the soul from *one*; yet much less that the *vis representativa universi* [representative force of the universe] could be assumed to be a base power. The proposition, however, that all the various actions of humans must be derived from the various powers of the soul serves to deal with the empirical psychology all the more systematically.

The Rational Psychology

Overview

In the rational psychology the human soul is recognised not from experience, as in the empirical psychology, but rather *from concepts a priori*. Here we shall examine *how much we can perceive of the human soul through reason*. The greatest desire of humans is not to know the actions of the soul which perceives through experience, but rather its future state. The individual clauses of the rational psychology are not as important here as the *general consideration of the soul, of its origin, of its future state and its persistence*. Here we must make an attempt at how much we are able to perceive of that through reason.

The concept of the soul in itself is a concept of experience. But in the rational psychology we take nothing more from experience than the mere concept of the soul, *that* we have a soul. The rest must be perceived from pure reason. That cognition where we left the main thread of experience is the *metaphysical cognition* of the soul.

The soul is accordingly considered from a three-fold point of view:

---

*   [Tr.: see 15 f.]

1. *absolute*; *simply in and of itself*, according to its subject, from mere pure concepts of reason alone. The first part thus comprises in itself the absolute consideration of the soul. This is the *transcendental* part of the rational psychology.
2. In *comparison with other things overall*, either with bodies, or with other thinking natures external to it, to the extent it distinguishes itself from the corporeal natures, and conforms with the thinking natures. In the first case we are investigating whether the soul is material or immaterial; and in the second, how far it conforms with the souls of animals, or other higher spirits.
3. In respect to *the connection of the soul with other things*, and indeed, because it belongs to the concept of the soul that it is connected with a body; thus of the connection of the soul with the body, or of the *commerce* between them both. Here now the following are dealt with:
   a. Of the *possibility* of this *commerce*;
   b. Of the *beginning* of the connection of the soul with the body, or of our birth;
   c. Of the *end* of this connection of the soul with the body, or of the state of the soul at our death. With the beginning of the connection, the state of the soul *before* the connection is examined; whether that takes place? And finally at the occasion of death, or with the end of the connection, the state of the soul *after* the connection is examined, also whether there will be a continuation of it? This thus hangs together in such a way quite well.

But while we consider the soul according to these three parts, some material must yet be brought in. If we namely consider in the first section the soul *absolutely*, thus from transcendental concepts of ontology, then we will examine, e.g. whether the soul is a substance or an accident; whether it is simple or composite; whether a single soul or whether many souls are in the human (unity is not always identical with simplicity); whether it is a *Substantia spontanea* [spontaneous substance], or whether it is necessitated from

44

without. Thus here it will be about the *transcendental free-dom*, whether the soul is a being which is independent, and is not necessitated by anything. All this is dealt with and proven in the first section.

When we deal in the second section with the *comparison* of the soul with other things, then there the immateriality is shown — that the soul is not only a simple substance, but also distinct from all the simple parts of the body. Furthermore, in *comparison with thinking natures*, the degree of its perfection is shown; how far it goes above the animal's soul, and how far it stands under the perfection of higher spirits. This part can, however, only be dealt with *hypothetically*; i.e. it shows what is probably to be thought of and realised here through reason.

In the third section, where the *connection* is dealt with, and indeed from its beginning, the state of the soul *before* the connection is considered and looked into — whether we can realise something of it using concepts with reason. Here we will, however, see that our transcendental concepts do not go any further than experience leads us, and that they only direct cognition *a posteriori*. We can indeed arrive *as far as the bounds* of experience, both *a parte ante* [before birth] and *post* [after], but *not past the bounds* of experience. Only here we will philosophise with profit in that we thereby keep within limits the false sophistry which only undermines true cognition. We will *not* talk here *dogmatically* of the state of the soul before birth and after death; *although you can talk far more about what you know nothing of than about what you know something about*. Accordingly we will determine here the limits of human reason so that false sophistry under the appearance of rational cognition cannot undermine our true principles in view of the practical.

First section of the rational psychology

When in the transcendental part of the rational psychology we consider the soul *absolutely*, we apply the transcendental concepts of ontology to it.

These are:

1. that the soul is a substance;
2. that it is simple;

3. that it is a single substance; and
4. that it is *simpliciter spontanea agens* [simply acting spontaneously].

These are the transcendental concepts according to which we consider the soul.

When I talk about the soul, I talk of the ego *in sensu stricto* [in the strict sense]. We receive the concept of the soul only through *the ego*; thus through the inner consideration of the inner mind in that I am conscious of all my thoughts so that I accordingly can talk of myself as a state of the inner mind. This object of the inner mind, *this subject, the consciousness in sensu stricto*, is the soul. *In sensu stricto* I take the self, to the extent I leave out everything which *in sensu latiori* [in a wider sense] belongs to my self. The ego *in sensu latiori*, however, expresses me as the entire human with soul and body. The body, however, is an object of the external senses. I can perceive any individual part of the body through the external senses, just like all other objects. The soul is, however, an object of the inner mind. To the extent I now feel myself to be an object and am conscious of that, this signifies the ego *in sensu stricto* or the self-ness just by itself, the soul. We would not have this concept of the soul if we could not abstract from the object of the inner mind everything external; therefore the ego *in sensu stricto* does not express the entire human, but rather only the soul.

If we now talk of the soul *a priori*; we will say nothing more of it than to the extent we are able to derive everything from the concept of the ego, and to the extent we can utilise on this ego the transcendental concepts. And this is the *true philosophy of showing the source of cognition*; for else you could not know how I can know something about the soul *a priori*, and why transcendental concepts are not used anymore on it.

We will thus recognise from the soul *a priori* nothing more than just as much as the ego lets us recognise. But I recognise from the soul:

1. That it is a substance; or, I am a substance. The *ego* signifies the subject in so far as it is not a predicate of another thing. That which is not a predicate of another thing is a substance. The ego is *the general subject* of all predicates, all

thinking, all actions, all possible judgements which we can return from ourselves as a thinking being. I can only say: I am, I think, I act. It is thus absolutely not about the ego being a predicate of something else. I cannot be a predicate of another being; I am entitled indeed to predicates; only I cannot predicate the ego by another; I cannot say: a different being is the ego. Consequently the ego, or the soul which is expressed through the ego, is a substance.

2. The soul is *simple, i.e. the ego signifies a simple concept*. Many beings cannot taken together comprise an ego. When I say that I think, then I am not expressing ideas which are distributed amongst many beings, but rather I am expressing an idea which takes place with *one* subject. For all thoughts can only be simple or composite. One and the same simple thought can only take place in one simple subject. For if the parts of the ideas should be divided up amongst many subjects, then each subject would have only one part of the idea; therefore no single subject would have the idea entirely. But in order that the entire idea is in the subject entirely, all the parts of the idea would have to be in the one subject. For if they were not combined in the one subject, the idea would not be whole. For example, if the expression *Quidquid agis etc.* [whatever you do etc.] should be divided amongst many subjects so that each would have one part; if namely the word *Quidquid* was said into the ear of one, *agis* into that of another, so that nobody would have heard the entire saying, then you could not say that the entire thought is together in the many heads so that each has one part of the thought; but rather the thought is not at all, in that each has only the thought of one word, but not a part of the whole idea. Accordingly indeed many beings can have at the same time one and the same thought, but each has the thought entirely. Only many beings cannot together have *one* entire idea. Accordingly that subject which has an idea must be *simple*. The soul is thus either a simple substance, or a *Compositum* [composite] of substances. When it is the latter, then it cannot think at all. For even if a part thinks, all the parts cannot though have *one* thought together; thus a composite of substances, where there is a plurality of substances, cannot think at all; accordingly the soul must be a simple substance.

3. The soul is a *single soul* (the unity of the soul), i.e. *my consciousness is the consciousness of a single substance*. I am not conscious of several substances. For if several thinking beings were in the human, then you would also have to be conscious of several thinking beings. The ego, however, expresses the unity; I am conscious of *one* subject.

4. The soul is a being which acts *simpliciter* [simply] spontaneously; i.e. the *human soul is free in sensu transcendentali* [in a transcendental sense]. The practical or psychological freedom was the independence of the arbitrary from the necessitation of the *stimulorum* [stimuli]. This was dealt with in the empirical psychology, and this concept of freedom was also sufficiently enough for morality. Now follows, however, the transcendental *concept* of freedom; this signifies absolute spontaneity, and is self-activation from the *inner principle* according to the freely arbitrary. The *Spontaneitas* [spontaneity] is either *absoluta vel simpliciter talis* [absolutely or simply such], or *secundum quid talis* [in a certain sense such]. *Spontaneitas secundum quid* [Spontaneity in a certain sense] is when something acts spontaneously *under one condition*. Thus, for example, a body which is shot off moves spontaneously; but *secundum quid*. This *Spontaneitas* is also called *Spontaneitas automatica* [automatic spontaneity]; when namely a machine moves according to the inner principle of itself; e.g. a clock, a spit turner. Spontaneity is, however, not *simpliciter talis*, because there the inner principle was determined by a *Principium externum* [external principle]. The *Principium internum* [internal principle] with the clock is the spring, with the spit turner the weight; but the *Principium externum* is the artist who determines the *Principium internum*. The *Spontaneitas simpliciter talis* is an absolute spontaneity.

It is to be asked, however, do the actions of the soul, its thoughts, come from the inner principle which is not determined by any causes; or are its actions determined by a *Principium externum*? If the latter were the case, then it would only have *spontaneitatem secundum quid*, but not *simpliciter talem*, and thus no freedom in the transcendental mind. If it is assumed (which though is only agreed in the *Theologia rationali* [rational theology]) that the soul has a cause, that it is

48

a *ens dependens* [dependent being], a *causatum alterius* [something caused by another]; then here the question is whether the soul as a being which has a cause could have been bestowed *spontaneitas absoluta*. This is a difficulty which holds us here. Were it an *ens independens* [independent being], then we could think in it in any case *spontaneitatem absolutam*. But if I assume it is an *ens ab alio* [being from another]; then it seems to be very probable that it is also determined by this cause for all its thoughts and actions; thus only has *spontaneitatem secundum quid*; that it indeed acts freely according to the inner principle, but is determined by a cause. Now the question is whether I can think as soul. Whether I have *spontaneitatem transcendentalem* or *libertatem absolutam*.

Here the ego must help out again. It is true that the *spontaneitas absoluta* cannot be comprehended in an *ente dependente* by reason; the pure self-activation with a being which is a *causatum* [caused thing] cannot be looked into. *Only although the spontaneitas absoluta cannot be comprehended; it can thus also not be disproved.* Therefore we will only have to look at whether the ego can be dedicated to self-activation; whether I can act freely by myself without all the determinations of a cause. If I do something, do I do it myself, or does another work in me? If the latter happens, then I am not free, but rather determined by a cause outside me. If I do it, however, from an inner principle which is not determined by anything outside; then *spontaneitas absoluta* is in me in the transcendental mind. But the ego proves that I act myself; *I* am a principle and not a *Principiatum* [principality]; *I* am conscious of my determinations and actions; and such a subject who is conscious of his determinations and actions has *libertatem absolutam*. As a result of the subject having *libertatem absolutam*, because it is conscious, it proves that it is not *subjectum patiens* [an enduring subject], but rather *agens* [an agent]. Provided I am conscious of one of my active works; provided I act from the inner principle of the activity according to free arbitrariness, without an external determination; only then do I have *spontaneitatem absolutam*. When I say: I think, I act, etc.; then either the word I is affixed falsely, or I am free. If I were not free, then I could not say: *I* am doing it; but rather would have to say: I feel in myself a desire to do which someone has stimulated in me. But if I say: I am doing it; then that signifies a spontaneity *in sensu transcendentali*. But now if I am conscious that I can say: I am doing; I am consequently not conscious of any determination, and thus I am acting *absolutely freely*. Were I not free, but rather only a means by which the other does something *immediate* in me, which I do; then I could not *say*: I am doing. I am doing, as *actio* [action], cannot be used in any other way than *absolutely* freely. All practical objective sentences would have no meaning if the human were not free. All practical instructions would be useless; you could not then say: you should do this or that. Now there is, however, such imperatives according to which I should do something; therefore all practical sentences must assume both problematically and pragmatically and ethically a freedom in me; consequently I must be the *first cause* of all actions. But since we have proven in the empirical psychology practical freedom, according to which we are free of the *necessitatione a stimulus* [necessity by means of stimulus], then through that the practical leaps must be able to take place; therefore *morals are more secure in view of that, which is our primary aim.* But we must always think, we are in the *Psychologia rationali*; here we must not call on any experience, but rather from principles of pure reason demonstrate the *spontaneitatem absolutam*; *where I thus go beyond the practical*, and ask: how is such practical freedom, according to which I act from the inner principle, possibly determined by no external cause? Here it is thus not about the will; this can probably later be applied to the free will; but rather I use the ego or the *substratum* of all experience as the basis, and make of it pure transcendental predicates. Then I am in the *Psychologia rationali*. Ego or the soul has *spontaneitatem absolutam actionum* [absolute spontaneity of actions]. These are purely transcendental concepts. But to examine this sentence still further, we must yet leave it out until where the talk is of *divine freedom* in the *theologia naturali*. It becomes difficult still through the mind of speculation to understand how one could act like an *ens derivativum actus originarios* [being derived from the original act]; only the basis that we cannot understand it lies in our mind; *for we can never comprehend the beginning*, rather only what happens in the sequence of causes and effects. The beginning, however, is the boundary of the sequence, but freedom makes utterly new segments for a new beginning; for this reason it is difficult to understand. Just because the possibility of such freedom cannot be understood, it does not yet follow that because we do not understand it that there also cannot be any freedom. *Freedom* is, however, *a necessary condition of all our practical actions*. Just like there are other sentences which we do not understand, but which assume a necessary condition; thus we are also through the concept of transcendental freedom independent.

But it is to be asked whether there could be a *fatum stoicum* [stoic fate] according to which our actions which we freely name are necessary through the relationship to the uppermost cause, to the extent each member in the ordering is already defined? If this were so; then no imputation could be applied. For example, a stoic said he had to steal from his lord through fate; his lord, however, had him hung through fate. But this is sophistry; and although we cannot contradict fatalism; the other person cannot prove it. Here no way out is to be found in all cases; and we do well *if we come to a stop where we cannot go any further*. In respect to the practical, however, we cannot admit fatalism in that we find with ourselves that we are not determined by any cause for our actions. *Accordingly religion and morals remain in safety*. The concept of freedom is practically sufficient, but not speculatively. If we could explain the free original actions from reason; then the concept would be speculatively sufficient. But we cannot do this because free actions are those which arise from the inner principle of all actions without any determination of an external cause. Now we cannot understand how the soul can exert such actions. This difficulty is not an objection, but rather a subjective difficulty of our reason. An objection is an objective difficulty, but here reason has hindrances to understanding the matter. There the matter does not suffer anything in itself *if the difficulty lies within us*. Lacking here are the conditions under which reason can understand something; these are the determining grounds. Our free actions, however, have no determining grounds; thus we cannot understand them either. This is a basis for understanding the limits of the mind, but not for denying the matter. The subjective difficulty, however, is in respect to *our mind* just as if it were an objective difficulty; *although the subjective hindrances of the incomprehensibility are essentially different from the objective hindrances of the impossibility.*

Second section of the rational psychology

In the second section of the rational psychology the human soul is weighed in *comparison with other things.*

We consider, however, the soul here in comparison
1.   with corporeal natures, and
2.   with other thinking natures.

If we compare the soul as an object of the inner mind with the objects of the external senses; is it material, or immaterial? Is it an object of the external senses or of the inner mind? The ego indicates that I have no other concept of the soul than of an object of the inner mind. All objects of the external senses are material, I thereby become aware of the objects of the external senses when they are present in space through impenetrability. But I am conscious of the soul through the inner mind and not through the external senses; thus I understand that for me the soul is given as an object of the inner mind. Furthermore we see thus that all actions of the soul, the thinking, wanting, etc. are not objects of the external senses. A thinking being as such cannot be an object of the external senses at all; we can neither perceive the thinking, nor the wanting, nor the capability for lust and reluctance through the external senses; and we cannot imagine how the soul should as a thinking being be an object of the external senses; only that it is not then, so it is also not material. Were the soul an object of the external senses; then it would have to be such on the strength of the impenetrability in space; for by that we become aware only of objects through the external senses. But because we know the actions of the soul from the side which is not at all an object of the external senses; then the soul also must not be an object of the external senses, but rather it must be immaterial. This, however, we cannot claim so firmly and certainly either; but rather only so far as we know it.

But we have already demonstrated that the soul is a substance, and then that it is a simple substance. From that Wolff believed to be able to prove already the immateriality; only that is false; from the simplicity immateriality does not yet follow; for the smallest part of a body is really though something material and an object of the external senses. If it is not like any real object of the external senses; then it can though through the putting together of many such little parts become a perceptible object of the external senses. If thus the soul were also simple, then it could be material though; and if it were put together with other such simple parts, then it could become a real object of the external senses. For example, if we imagine a cubic inch were filled with matter, and you asked: if the soul is merely simple, would it have the space so that just such a simple part would have to be cleared away in whose place it should enter? Or would it have place in it without that having to happen? If the former is claimed; then it must follow that if I continue with the second, third, fourth, and following souls, I will have finally cleared away all the material from the cubic inch and have the entire cubic inch full of souls which were present in space through impenetrability without taking any space. The soul can thus always be simple and yet material. But what no object of the external senses is also does not have to be in the slightest degree something corporeal; and even if yet so many of such simple pieces were put together, it does not have to be any perceptible object of the external senses, for it is material.

What is now the source of this knowledge? (To the source of knowledge the philosopher must always return; this is better than if he knows all proofs by heart). *From what* can a philosopher prove the immateriality of the soul, and *how far* can he go? He can get the ideas from nothing else other than the expression *ego* which express the object of the inner mind. Thus immateriality lies in the concept of the ego. — We *cannot prove a priori* the immateriality of the soul, but rather *only so much as that all the characteristics and actions of the soul are not to be recognised from materiality.* Only these characteristics do not prove though that our soul shall have nothing external; rather only so much that I cannot assume materiality as a basis for explanation of actions. I rule out thus only materiality. For if I shall assume it; then I would re-cognise nothing anymore of the soul. You must hence not as-sume materiality arbitrarily; *but I have one basis for that of immateriality.* You could here already deceive someone and prove materiality from whether it follows directly from it. Only you have though a basis for immateriality, and that is this: everything which comprises a part of the whole of the space is between two bounds. The bounds of the space are the points; what is between two points is in the space; what is in the space is divisible; accordingly there is no simple part of the material, but rather all the material is in the space, and thus divisible as far as infinity. If now the soul were material; then it would have to at least be a simple part of the material, (because it has already been proven that the soul is simple). But now no part of the material is simple; for that is a contra-diction; thus even the soul is not material, but immaterial.

Now we consider the soul *in comparison with thinking natures* and indeed its agreement with animal souls and with other spirits. From the concept of the immateriality of the soul you have arrived at the concept of spirits. An immaterial being which is considered separate from all material, and can think for itself, is a *spirit.* In such a way the concept and the doctrine of spirits has come into psychology. The course which we have taken in considering the soul is this: that we showed the soul is a substance; a simple and freely acting substance; an immaterial substance. Now the question is: *is the soul also a spirit?* For to be a spirit it not only requires that it be an immaterial being, but rather that it also be a be-ing thinking for itself separate from all material. — If I re-gister my immaterial being with the name *soul*; then from the meaning of the word it follows that it is a being which stands not only in connection, but also in *commercio* [communica-tion] with a body. *If now this being is separated from the body; then the name soul also ceases.* Now it is to be asked: is the soul merely a material being which you can only think of as in *commercio* with the body; *or is it a spirit* which can also be thought of as separate from the body? It will not be invest-igated here whether it is now really that, but rather whether it has a means (irregardless that it now stands in *commercio* with the body) of also thinking without coexistence with it; that is, whether it, even separate from the body, can endure and live as a spirit? We will thus compare the human soul which is bound with the body with beings which stand in no coexistence at all with bodies, and *those are spirits*; or with such beings which stand in the same coexistence as the human soul with the body, which are beings who have mere sensoriality and power of imagination; and those are *animal souls*. We will thus talk:

a) *de anima bruti* [of the soul of the animal], whose coexistence depends on the body;

b) *de spiritu* [of the spirit], which is in no coexistence at all with the body; and

c) *de anima humana* [of the soul of the human], of which we have already principally spoken about previously, which indeed stands in coexistence with the body, but is independent in that it can also live and think without the body as a spirit.

But if we compare the soul of the human with animal souls and with other spirits; then you do not have to hope here to hear many secrets and discoveries which nobody else knows, and which the philosopher would have drawn from a secret source; but you will have expected one discovery here though, which cost much effort, and which yet few know — namely *the limits of reason and of philosophy to understand* how far reason can go here. We will thus get to know here *our ignorance*, and understand *the basis for it*: why it is impossible that in this no philosopher can go further, and also will not give further; and *if we know that, then we already know a lot*.

Animals are not merely machines or matter, but rather they have souls; for everything in all of nature is either lifeless or animated. All matter as matter (*materia, qua talis*) is lifeless. From where do we know that? The concept which we have of matter is this: *materia est extensum impenetrabile iners* [matter is inert, impenetrable expanse]. When we, for example, perceive a mote of dust on the paper; then we are seeing whether it moves. If it does not move by itself; then we consider it to be lifeless matter which is *inert*, and which might remain lying for all eternity if it were not moved by something else. But as soon as the matter moves; then we see whether it moves arbitrarily by itself. When we become aware of that in the mote of dust; we say thus it is *animated*; it is *an animal.* An animal is thus an animated matter; for life is the means of defining itself from the inner principle arbitrarily. Matter, however, as matter, has no inner principle of self-activation, no spontaneity to move itself; rather all matter which is animated has an inner principle which is separate from the object of the external senses, and is an object of the inner mind. An inner principle of self-activation is only thinking and wanting; only through that can something be moved through the inner mind; this is alone a principle of acting as you like and arbitrarily. If matter thus moves; then it follows that in it there is such a special principle of self-activation. This principle, however, of thinking and wanting is something only a being which has knowledge is capable of. Matter can merely move by means of such a principle. Such a principle of matter, however, is the soul of the material. Thus: all matter which then lives does not live as matter, but rather has a principle of life and is animated. But to the extent matter is animated; to that extent it is also *possessing a soul.* A principle of life lies thus at the basis of animals and that is the soul.

With these souls of the animals and our souls, we should draw a comparison *a priori* without any experience and see what the difference consists of; only if we should recognise beings which have the power of imagination, and indeed *a priori*; where do we receive the distinctions from, where they are not given to us at all? We should recognise souls which are external to us, and for which we have no data at all? Only this distinction and the data for it we take again from ourselves and from our concept of the ego. We know our soul merely through the inner mind; but we also have an external sense; accordingly all distinction will rest merely on our external sense and inner mind. If we imagine *a priori* beings; then we will not notice the distinctions by degree, but rather by species; thus the distinction and the comparison must rest on our external sense and inner mind. Accordingly we can imagine beings which have a capability of the external senses, but dispense with the capabilities of the inner mind, and those are the animals.

Accordingly the animals will have all the suggestions of the external senses; they will dispense only with that suggestion which rests on the inner mind, which rests on the consciousness of itself, in short on the concept of the ego. They will accordingly have no understanding and no reason; for all actions of the mind and of reason are possible only in so far as you are conscious of yourself. They will have no general knowledge through reflection, nor the identity of the ideas, nor even the connections of the ideas according to the subject and predicate, according to cause and effect, according to the whole and the parts; for those are all consequences of the consciousness which the animal is lacking.

We can attribute to animals an *Analogon rationis* [analogue of reason], which are linkages of ideas according to the laws of sensoriality, from which the same effects follow as from the linking according to concepts. Animals are accordingly not to be distinguished by degree from the human soul, but rather by species; for if the animal soul increases in its sensory capabilities ever so much, the consciousness of itself, the inner mind, can though not be achieved thereby. Even if they exercise directly in their sensoriality better phenomena than we do; they are lacking though the inner mind.

Since we have concluded from the nature of the spirit that everything which is a principle of life must also live; we must grant such also to the souls of animals. Accordingly, just as our intellectuality will increase in the other world; so too can the sensoriality increase with animals, but they will never compare with us. Now we can think it problematic that such beings exist which have no inner mind; for it is no contradiction to assume such. How many phenomena with such beings as have no inner mind now are to be explained by the capabilities of external sensoriality without assuming an inner mind? The consciousness of oneself, the concept of the ego, does not take place with such beings as have no inner mind; accordingly no irrational animal can think: I am; from this follows the distinction that beings which have such a concept of the ego possess *personality*.

This is the physical personality provided they can say: I am. Furthermore it follows that such beings have *freedom*, and everything can be imputed to them; and this is the *practical personality* which has consequences in ethics. But if you wanted to cite phenomena which is to be explained merely by the external sensoriality; then you could explain here quite well the entire empirical psychology of animals. Because this, however, is intertwined with physics, we would digress too far thereby from the *Psychologia rationali*. But we see actions undertaken by animals which we would not be able to bring about except by understanding and reason. Accordingly the sensoriality is with us such a state as with animals; but that theirs is far more advanced than ours. We have, however, substituted for this loss through the consciousness of ourselves, and through the understanding which follows from that. Also we are not required at all to assume with animals reflection, but rather we can derive all this from the formative power. We allocate accordingly to these beings a capability for sentience, imagination, etc., but all only sensorially as lower capability and not connected with consciousness. From this external sensoriality and for mechanical reasons of their body, we can explain all the phenomena of animals without assuming consciousness or the inner mind. The philosopher must not increase the principles of knowledge without cause.

Since we have now compared our soul with beings who are *below* it; we want now to compare it also with beings which are *above* it. Since we have external senses and inner mind, and we can imagine beings which have merely an external sense; we can also imagine on the other hand beings which have no external sense at all, which do not fall into the senses at all, and which are thus immaterial. Accordingly we can imagine immaterial beings who are gifted with consciousness of themselves. An immaterial thinking being which is gifted with consciousness (from which it then follows that it is also a rational being) is a spirit. From the spirit must be distinguished that which it is *spiritual. Spiritual beings* are those which are indeed connected with the body, but which can continue their ideas, their thinking and wanting even if they are separated from the body. Now it is to be asked: is the soul of the human a spiritual being? — If it can also continue to

58

live without the body, then it is spiritual and if the souls of animals can also do such, then they are also of a spiritual nature. But a spirit which is really separated from the body is one which, without being an object of the external senses, can nevertheless think and want. What can we now recognise about the spirits *a priori? We can only think of spirits problematically, i.e. no reason can be a priori derived for rejecting them.* Experience teaches us that when we think our body comes into play, but we do not see that it is necessary. We can imagine quite well beings which have no body and nevertheless can think and want. Accordingly we can assume problematically thinking rational beings with consciousness of themselves who are immaterial. Something can be assumed to be problematic if it is plainly clear that it is *possible.* We cannot prove it beyond dispute, but nobody can disprove either that such spirits should not exist. Likewise we cannot demonstrate the existence of God beyond dispute; but nobody is in a position either to prove to me the opposite, for where does he want to derive that from?

Now we can say nothing more about these spirits than what a spirit which is separate from a body can do. They are not a object of the external senses; thus they are not in space. *We cannot say anything further here; otherwise we fall into fantasies.* The concept of animal souls and of higher spirits is only a play on our concepts. The result is: we learn of ourselves that we are an object of the external senses and inner mind. Now we can imagine beings which have merely an external sense, and they are animal souls; but we can also imagine beings which merely have an inner mind, and those are spirits. When we imagine beings which have both an inner mind and external senses; then they are *human souls.*

We cannot prove by this anything, but rather only assume it to be problematic in that the impossibility of it cannot be demonstrated. Luckily experience teaches us yet that there really are such beings of which we say in the *Psychologia rationali* that they only have merely an external sense; but that there are beings which merely have an inner mind, *about them it is impossible for experience to enlighten us.*

Third section of the rational psychology

In the third section of the rational psychology the *linkages of the soul with other things* is treated.

We deal first with the *linkage of the soul with the body*, or of the *commercio* between both.

A *commercium* is a reciprocal determination. The dependency of the determination which is not reciprocal is not a *commercium*, but rather a *connection*. God stand in such a one-sided connection with the world. The *commercium* between soul and body is, however, a reciprocal dependency of the determination. We ask accordingly at first: how is such a *commercium* between a thinking being and a body possible? (Between the soul and the body I cannot say; for the concept of the soul assumes already a *commercium*.) The basis of understanding the difficulty of this *commercium* rests on that the soul is an object of the inner mind and the body is an object of the external senses. In the body I do not become aware of anything mental, and in the soul I do not become aware of anything external. Now it is not to be comprehended through any reason how that which is an object of the inner mind should be a basis of that which is an object of the external senses. Thinking and wanting are merely objects of the inner mind. Were thinking and wanting a moving force; then it would be an object of the external senses themselves. But because now thinking and wanting are merely objects of the inner mind (thus a basis of the inner determination); it is difficult to understand how such can be a basis of the external determination. And since on the other hand the movement as an object of the external senses is a basis of the external determination; it is thus difficult to determine how then this can be a basis of the inner determinations and ideas. The reciprocal determination between thinking and wanting and between movements is something we cannot understand through reason. *The impossibility of understanding such things through reason does not at all prove, however, the inner impossibility of the thing itself.* But we can understand it through experience; and this does not indeed only work this way here, but all basic powers are given to us through experience and none are to be understood through reason. We are thus familiar in the body only with those powers whose effects are phenomena of the external senses; and in the soul we are familiar with no other powers than those whose effects arc phenomena of the inner mind. Now how the powers of the external senses of the body can be the basis of the phenomena of the soul and how the powers of the soul can be the basis of the phenomena of the body cannot be understood at all. Only not only is the *commercium* between the soul and the body difficult to understand, but also the *commercium* between the bodies amongst themselves. We can indeed understand; but only if we already assume powers of *commercii* beforehand. This basic power of the *commercii* amongst the bodies cannot be understood by any being whose reason is not intuitive, but rather discursive. For all *Systemata explicandi commercium animae corpore* [systems explaining the interaction of the soul with the body] are yet fruitless and in vain; for no system can explain how movement arises from thinking and conversely how thinking arises from movement, because you cannot understand any basic power. You have already philosophised enough when you just *arrive at the basic power*. All *Systemata explicandi commercium* [systems explaining interaction] lead to it because they see the inequality between thinking and movement. Hence they artificially make things up in every way, because they imagine that the natural influence is impossible. Only in view of the soul do the phenomena show that the will has an influence on the body, and conversely, that the soul has a power to move the body. But we can provide no basis for that; for that is a basic power, a basic means. Accordingly the *commercium* is, because it happens according to specific laws, a natural influence, and the coexistence is natural. Because it was believed the *commercium* cannot possibly be natural; you have brought a third being into play and said, like Leibniz, either God already has in the beginning arranged the actions of the soul and of the body so that they agree; or like Descartes, that God arranges at every opportunity the actions of both so that they agree. But we cannot understand both the *commercium* between the bodies amongst themselves and that between the soul and the body in any other way than that it is possible, to the extent all substances are there through *one*; for that reason they stand in coexistence. *How* this is between the soul and the body, however, is not to be understood.

Now since the soul stands in *commercio* with the body; we ask: where does the soul have its seat in the body? The place of the soul in the world is determined by the place of the body; *my soul is there where my body is*. But where does the soul have its seat in the body? The place of the body in the world is only determined by the *external* sense; since now the soul is an object of the *inner* mind, through the inner mind, however, no place can be determined: thus *the place of the soul in the body cannot be determined either*; for through the inner actions no external circumstance can be defined. The soul, however, sees only by the inner mind; thus it cannot see itself in a place and be conscious of a place. I cannot feel in the body the place where the soul sits; for otherwise I would have to see by an external sense; but I see myself by the inner mind. As little as an eye can see itself; as little can the soul see externally. But it can be conscious of external parts of the body, principally those which contain the most fruitful causes of its sensations. The cause of all sensations, however, is the nervous system. Without the nerves we could not feel anything external. The root of all nerves is, however, the brain; with every feeling accordingly the brain is stimulated because in the brain all nerves are concentrated. Thus the soul must set the seat *of its sensations* in the brain as the *place of all stipulation* of feelings. *But that is not the place of the soul itself*, but rather the place from which all nerves, and consequently all feelings arise. We find that the brain harmonises with all actions at the mercy of the soul. I feel every part especially. If I, for example, hold my finger in the fire, then I feel there the pain; but in the end all feelings of any particular part of the body concentrate themselves in the brain, the stem of all nerves; for if the nerves of one part of the body are cut off, then we will certainly feel nothing of that part. Accordingly the principle of all feelings must be in the brain. Now one imagines the soul has its seat there in the brain so that it can move all the nerves and be able to be affected again by the nerves. Only we do not though feel the seat of the soul in the brain, but rather the brain with all its changes harmonises with the soul. For example, pondering hurts the head. We do not indeed see the place, but rather only conclude that the brain is the seat of the soul because the soul mostly has an affect there. If we imagine a place in the brain which is the first principle of the stem of the nerves, where all the nerves run together and end in one point which is called the *sensorium commune* [common seat of sensation], but which no doctor has seen; then it is to be asked now: does the soul sit in this *sensorio communi*? Has it taken up a small place there so that it can direct from there the entire body and as it were like an organist direct from one place the entire body; or has it no place at all in the body, so that the body itself is its place? Assuming that the soul would not have taken up a little place in the brain where it plays on our nerves like an organ; then we could believe that, if we were to go through all the parts of the body, we would have to come in the end to the place where the soul sits. If you were to now take away this place; the entire human might indeed still be there, but it would be missing the place where the organist as it were is supposed to play on the organ; this is, however, meant very materialistically. But if the soul is not an object of the external senses; then it will also not be entitled to the conditions for external contemplation. The condition of external contemplation, however, is space. Since it now is not an object of external contemplation; it is also *not in space*, but rather it only has effects in space — and although we say *analogice* [analogically], it is in space, we must not take this though physically. Just like you say that God is in a church. Accordingly we claim the second, namely: the soul does not have a special place in the body; its place is, however, determined in the world by the body and is connected directly with the body. The possibility of this *commercii* we do not understand; we must, however, not only set the conditions of this *commercii*, how they are amongst themselves with the bodies, namely through impenetrability, for otherwise it becomes material. To allocate a place in the body for it is absurd and materialistic.

Now we will consider *the soul with the body*, over time, in *commercio*; and indeed the state of the soul in the *beginning* of the *commercii*, or with the *birth*; in the *commercio* itself, or in *life*; and at the *end* of the *commercii*; or at the *death*.

Life consists of the *commercio* of the soul with the body; the beginning of the life is the beginning of the *commercii*, the end of the life is the end of the *commercii*. The beginning of the *commercii* is the birth, and the end of the *commercii* is the death. The duration of the *commercii* is the life. The beginning of life is the birth; but this is not the beginning of the life of the soul, but rather of the human. Birth, life, and death are thus only *states* of the soul; for the soul is a simple substance; thus it also cannot be produced when the body is produced, and will also not be dissolved when the body is dissolved; *for the body is only the form for the soul*. The beginning or the birth of the human is thus only the beginning of the *commercii*, or the altered state of the soul; and the end or the death of the human is only the end of the *commercii*, or the altered state of the soul. Only the beginning of the *commercii* or the birth of the human is not the beginning of the principle of the life, and the end of the *commercii* or the death of the human is not the end of the principle of the life; for the principle of the life does not arise through the birth, and does not stop through the death. The principle of the life is a simple substance. From the substantiality or simplicity, however, it does not follow at all that the birth of the human is the beginning of the substance, and the death of the human the end of the substance; for a simple substance does not arise and decay according to the laws of nature. Therefore the substance remains, even if the body decays; and thus the substance must also have been present when the body arose. — The substance always remains unchanged; accordingly the birth, the life, and the death are only various states of the soul. A state *though assumes already an existence*; for the beginning is not a state, the birth is, however, a state of the soul, thus not a beginning of the soul.

Since we have considered the state of the soul at the beginning of the *commercii*; we must now consider the soul *before* the beginning of the connection, or its state before the birth, and *after* the end of the connection, or its state after the death. Between the state of the soul before the birth and after the death there is a great agreement. For if the soul had not lived before the union with the body, then we could not conclude that it will also live after the union with it. For if it had arisen with the body; then it could also cease with the body. For that which shall be after the union, it can also have been *for just the same reasons* before the union. But we can also conclude from the state after the death, which we will prove, the state before the birth; for it *seems to flow* from the proofs which we will give for the persistence of the soul after the death that we were *before* the birth in the pure spiritual life; and that through the birth the soul, so to say, has arrived in a dungeon, in a cave which hinders it in its spiritual life. Only here there is the question of whether the soul in its spiritual life before the birth had complete use of its powers and capabilities; whether it possessed all the knowledge, the experience of the world, or whether it obtained it firstly through the body? We answer: It does not at all follow from the soul having been before the birth in a purely spiritual life that it had in that life such a complete use of its powers and capabilities, and even the same knowledge of the world (which it only attained after the birth); rather it follows instead that the soul had been in a spiritual life, had a spiritual power of life, possessed all the abilities and capabilities already; but in such a way that all these abilities were only developed through the body, and that it only obtained all the knowledge which it has of the world through the body, and thus must have prepared itself through the body for the future persistence. *The state of the soul before the birth was thus without consciousness of the world and of itself.*

About the State of the Soul after the Death

Now we want to consider the state of the soul after the death. Here we have two questions to pose:
1) whether the soul will live and persist after death, and
2) whether it by its nature must live and persist. That is, whether it is immortal.

If the soul lives; then it does not yet follow that it, by its nature, must necessarily live; for it could indeed be kept alive by God from certain intentions of reward or improvement. But then, if it only lived *accidentally*; then the time could come where it could stop living. But if it *by its nature* were immortal; then it would have to *in a necessary way* persist forever. Accordingly we will not have to prove here the *acci-*

dental life of the soul (that it will merely live follows already from its substantiality in that every substance persists, even the substance of the body; for if the wood is burned, only the parts are dissolved, the substance though remains forever), but rather that it is *immortal. Immortality is the natural necessity to live.* To prove this has far more in itself than the mere accidental life which can be demonstrated with many proofs, from justness, wisdom, goodness, etc. of God. That proof, however, which is derived from nature and the concept of the matter itself, is every time the only possible proof, and it is *transcendental.* Many proofs of a matter cannot be given *a priori.* The other proofs for the immortality of the soul which you otherwise have are not proofs for its immortality, but rather they prove only the *hope* of the future life. The proof for the immortality of the soul which is derived from nature and from the concept rests on that life is nothing more than a capability of acting from the *inner* principle, from the spontaneity. Now it already lies in the general concept of the soul that it is a subject. Spontaneity contains in itself determining itself from the inner principle. It is the source of the life which animates the body. Because now all matter is lifeless (for that is the concept which we have of matter in that we are not familiar with any other); everything which belongs to life cannot be derived from matter. The act of spontaneity cannot derive from the external principle; that is, there cannot be external causes of life; for otherwise there would not be spontaneity in life. That lies already in the concept of life, since it is a capability of determining actions from the *inner* principle. Thus no body can be the cause of life. For because the body is matter, but all matter is lifeless; so the body is no basis for life, but rather more a hindrance to living which is resisting the principle of life. The basis of life must rather lie in another substance, namely in the soul; a basis which, however, rests not in the connection with the body, but rather in the inner principle of its spontaneity. Accordingly neither the beginning of the life of the soul, nor the persistence of the life of it will originate from the body. If the body thus stops straightaway; the principle of life still remains which exercised independently from the body the acts of life, and thus

66

also now, after the separation from the body, must exercise the same acts of life unhindered.

Life with humans is *twofold*: the animal and the spiritual life. The animal life is the life of the human as human; and here the body is necessary so that the human lives. The other life is the spiritual life where the soul, independently from the body, must continue to exercise the same acts of life. For the animal life the body is necessary; there the soul is in connection with the body; it has an effect on the body and animates it. If now the machine of the body is destroyed, so that the soul can no longer have an effect on it; then indeed the animal life ceases, but not the spiritual. Only you can say that all actions of the soul, e.g. thinking, wanting, etc., happen by means of the body which exhibits the experience; thus the body is the condition for the life of the soul. Certainly for as long as the spirit represents the soul, as long as the spirit stands in *commercio* with the body; for as long are the actions of the soul dependent upon the body; for otherwise there would be no *commercium*. As long as the animal lives, the soul is the principle of life; but the body is the instrument, the organon* by which the living acts of the soul are exercised in the world. If we thus consider two substances in *commercio*; it can certainly not be any other way than that the one substance is a condition of the other. Hence, for example, the soul cannot think if the body is ill. All sensory knowledge rests on the body, for it is the organon of the senses. As long as the human lives, the soul must be able to present its sensory ideas through the brain as if copied onto a slate.

Here it is about a soul which is connected to the body like with a human who is fastened to a cart. If this human moves, then the cart must move. But nobody will claim that the movement originates from the cart; just as the actions do not originate from the body, but rather from the soul. As long as the human is fastened to the cart, this is the condition of its movement. When he is freed from it, then he will be able to move more easily; thus this was a hindrance to his movement. But so long as he is still bound to it; for so long does the movement become easier, the better the instrument is able. If

---

*   [Tr.: instrument of thought.]

now the soul is already bound to the body; then the change to the hindrance is the conveying of life; just like how the movement is easier when the wheels of the cart are greased, although it would be even easier after the freeing from the cart. Thus a good constitution of the body is also a conveying of life, so long as the soul is bound to the body, although the conveying of life would be still better after the freeing from the body. For since the body is lifeless matter; it is a hindrance to life. But so long as the soul is bound to the body, it must bear this hindrance and seek in every way to relieve itself. If now, however, the body ceases completely; then the soul is freed from its hindrance and only now does it begin to live properly. Thus death is not the absolute abolition of life, but rather a freeing of the hindrance to a complete life. This lies already in the understanding of everyone and in the nature of the matter. The consciousness of the mere ego proves that life lies not in the body, but rather in a special principle which is different from the body; that consequently this principle can also persist without body, and through that its life is not diminished, but rather increased. *This is the only proof which can be given a priori* which is derived from the knowledge and the nature of the soul which we understood *a priori*.

Now we can conduct another proof *a priori*, but from the knowledge of another being.

What being do we know, however, *a priori*? We recognise the existence of our soul indeed from experience, but nature itself we understand *a priori*. That being which we can recognise *a priori* must be absolutely necessary. I can only recognise incidental beings through experience; I would know nothing of those if they were not given; but what is necessary, of that I understand *a priori* that it must be absolutely necessary. This absolutely necessary being is the divine being. If we now want to conclude from the necessity of this divine being the immortality of the soul, then we cannot *a priori* recognise that from the divine nature; for otherwise the soul would have to be a part of the divine nature. If I cannot thus recognise it from the nature of the being of the soul, what is then left? Answer: *freedom*; for nature and freedom are only that which can be recognised in a being. Accordingly we will conclude from the knowledge of the divine being the necessary persistence of the soul. This is the moral or (because the knowledge of God appears) the theological-moral proof. It rests on that all our actions stand under practical rules of obligation. This practical rule is the sacred moral law. This law we understand *a priori*, it lies in the nature of the actions that they should be thus and no different, which we understand *a priori*. It depends here, however, principally upon the dispositions that they are adequate with the sacred law where the *basis for motion* is also moral. All morality, however, exists in the quintessence of *the rule*, according to which we *become worthy to be happy* if we act according to it. It is not a directive of actions by which we *become* happy, but rather only by which we become *worthy* of blessedness. It teaches only the *conditions* under which the blessedness is possible to attain. These conditions, this law I understand through reason. But now in this world there is no path for attaining blessedness through these actions. We see that the actions by which we make ourselves worthy of blessedness cannot obtain the blessedness for us here. How often must probity not languish? Through honesty you do not get ahead at court. But since I now understand the law, but on the other hand have no promise at all, and cannot hope at all that my actions, if they are adequate to this law, will ever be rewarded; since I understand that I have made myself worthy by having followed this law, but cannot hope at all on the other hand to ever be blessed with this blessedness; all moral laws have no power; they are deficient because they cannot obtain that which they promise. It seems to be better that you do not endeavour at all to live adequately for this law, but rather seek to promote your happiness in the world as much as possible. In this way the cleverest rogue is the happiest if he knows only to make himself so clever that he is not caught; and the one who strives to live according to the moral law would be a right fool if he put behind himself the advantages in the world and snatched after such things which the moral law promises him, but cannot provide.

Here theology or the knowledge of God now assists. I understand an absolutely necessary being which is in a position to provide me that blessedness which I have made myself worthy of through observation of the moral law. But since now I see that this blessedness which I have made myself worthy of cannot be provided at all in this world, but rather quite often through my moral conduct and through my uprightness much of my temporal blessedness had to be sacrificed; there must thus be *another world, or a state, where the well-being of the creature will be adequate to the good behaviour of the same.* If now the human assumes another world; then he must also arrange his actions according to it, otherwise he is acting like a rascal. But if he does *not* assume the other world; then he would be acting like a fool if he wanted to arrange his actions to conform to the law which he understands through reason; for then the worst rascal would be the best and cleverest in that he sought only to promote his happiness here because he cannot hope for any future happiness.

This moral proof is practically sufficient enough for believing in a future state. The human with whom it should make its effect must *already beforehand* have taken on moral convictions; then such a one no longer needs any proof; he does not once hear the objections which are made; for him it is completely sufficient. It is the mainspring of virtue, and anyone who wanted to introduce the opposite would close all moral laws and all mainsprings to virtue; then the moral principles would only be chimeras. Only according to the speculation, according to the logical correctness, and according to its yardstick, this proof is *not sufficient* enough. For because we do not see that in this life vices are punished and virtues are rewarded; *it does not follow thus from that at all that there is another world*; for we cannot indeed know whether vices and virtues are not rewarded and punished here already. Everybody can indeed feel their punishment here; and even if their vices and crimes seem greater to us than they are punished; these crimes which we consider to be so punishable can indeed be according to the nature of their temperament even so human and even so small as with another who commits smaller crimes, but has a better nature of temperament and can sooner refrain from the vice. If we on the other hand do not see the virtuous so happy as he deserves to be; then perhaps his virtue was still quite tainted, and perhaps he does not thus deserve such a high blessedness. Furthermore you could interject: if we also assume that it is about a future so that each is rewarded and punished. — (You could here just as well ask: why do we not appear here already before the divine judge? Why must we die first? But if you wanted to get so deeply involved here in the question, then you could also ask: why does the horse not have six feet and two horns?) — Well, however, it is a future where each is rewarded and punished; so you are not permitted as a result to live eternally, in order that you be rewarded or punished. If each has received his reward or punishment; then it is at an end with him, and his life is over; for the relationship of crimes to the eternity of punishments is obviously too great, and even this also applies to the rewards; life can thus always stop if everything has already been rewarded and punished. Furthermore many people would not be permitted at all to appear before the divine seat of judgement merely because of rewards and punishments, in that they could have exercised neither good nor bad actions; as, for example, little children who died too early; savages who have no use for reason, and who do not know anything about any moral law. Thus according to this proof all people of that sort would not be permitted to assume any reckoning on a future life; and if the others were placed straightaway in the future state, they could though only remain there for as long as their rewards and punishments last.

Accordingly it is not enough that you prove the soul will live after the death; but rather it must also be proved that it by its nature must *necessarily* live; for otherwise, if I shall die only once, even if it should happen after several thousand centuries, I would prefer to die soon than spend a long time with the apprehensions and watching the comedy. —

Thus from this proof no necessary persistence can be demonstrated either. The previous proof, however, which was given from the nature of the soul and from the concept of the spirit, proves that the soul, by its spiritual nature, shall persist by necessity eternally. If now the soul, by its nature, is already *immortal*; then it applies to all, both little children and savages; for the nature of all souls is of the same kind. The moral proof is, however, a *sufficient basis of belief*. What can this belief produce though? The knowledge of a being which will reward and punish all actions according to this pure and sacred moral law. Anyone who believes that lives morally. The mere concept, however, cannot move them to it; accordingly this moral proof is practically sufficient for an honest man; a rascal, however, denies not only the law, but also its author.

The third proof is the empirical one which is derived from the psychology. It is taken from the nature of the soul, *to the extent it is derived from the experience*. We are attempting namely whether we cannot derive a proof from the experience which we have of the nature of the soul. — We notice from the experience that the powers of the soul increase just like the powers of the body, and decline just like the powers of the body. But it does not yet at all follow from it that if the body declines, and ceases completely, that the soul also ceases entirely with it. The body is indeed the condition of the animal life; accordingly the animal life indeed ceases, but not yet the entire life. Only this empirical proof cannot yet at all demonstrate *the immortality* of the soul. The general basis for why we cannot demonstrate from the observations and experiences of the human disposition the future persistence of the soul without the body is because all these experiences and observations happen *in connection with the body*. We cannot draw on any experiences in life except in connection with the body. Accordingly these experiences cannot prove what we can do *without* the body; for they have indeed happened *with* the body. If the human could be disembodied, the experience which it might then draw on could prove what it would be *without* the body. Since now such experience, however, is not possible, you also cannot demonstrate without this experience what the soul without the body will be. But this empirical proof has a *negative* use in that we namely can from experience make no certain conclusion *against* the life of the soul; for from that the body ceases it does not follow indeed yet at all that the soul will also cease. — No opponent can thus invent an argument *from experience* which demonstrates the mortality of the soul. Thus the immortality of the soul is at least secured against all objections which are derived from the experience.

The fourth proof is empirical-psychological, but from cosmological grounds; and this is the analogical proof. Here the immortality of the soul is concluded from the analogy of all of nature. — Analogy is the proportion of concepts where I work out from the relationship of two members which I know, in relationship to the third member which I know, the relationship of the fourth member which I do *not* know. The proof in itself is as follows. In all of nature we find that no powers, no capabilities, no tools reach either inanimate or animate beings which are not aimed at a specific *use* or *aim*. But we find in the soul such powers and capabilities which have in this life no specific aim; thus these capabilities must (since nothing is without use or aim in nature), if they have no use and specific aim here, have a use though *somewhere*; there must thus be a state where the powers can be used. Thus it is to be suspected of the soul that it must be kept for a future world where it can use all these powers it has. If we go through this sentence piece by piece; then we find through experience in all of nature that all animals do not have any organs, any powers and capabilities in vain, but rather that they all have their uses and specific aim. Now it is to be asked whether the powers of the human soul are so created that their use only stretches to this world; or whether also in it are abilities and capabilities which have here in this life no use and specific aim at all. If we investigate this; then we will find the latter confirmed. We need only take the soul's cognitive faculty, and we see that this stretches much further than the needs of life and the stipulations of this world demand. This is proven by a few sciences. Mathematics shows that our cognitive faculties stretch far above the bounds of our local destiny. We possess a desire to know which is up with the entire edifice of creation; we make observations with much effort; our desire to know stretches to every bright point of the heavens, as astronomy proves. Now it is to be asked whether all these efforts which consist in the gratification of our desire for knowledge have the slightest use for our present life. It is not at all very well-known that all the sciences by which we gratify our desire for knowledge do not have the slightest use for our life in this world; in that many nations exist who know nothing at all of them, who are very indifferent to the Copernican system, and who are quite well content with the lack of this insight. You can always live without such sciences; indeed the most important point of astronomy is directly of the least interest. The calendar and marine navigation would probably be the best uses which we have of them in the world; only you could even live without that if you should live nothing more than *only* here. These are also the consequences of the luxury of understanding which is not aimed at this life. We can after all live without the luxury of achieving ship's travel. The worth of our person does not exist in that we adorn ourselves with goods and clothes from foreign parts of the world; thus this also does not have an aim destined for this life. Our desire for knowledge, however, stretches yet further. The human investigates and asks: what was he before birth? What will he be after death? He goes even further and asks: where does the world come from? Is it infinite, or incidental, or of eternity, and has it a cause? How is this cause obtained? All this knowledge does not interest me at all in this life. If I were only for this world alone, what need do I have to know: where I am or the world is from, and who the cause of this world is, and how it is obtained; if I am just there and and can live. Since now all these capabilities cannot be in vain; they must have their use in another state. Even those aims which can be the most interesting in this life, e.g. how a good beer etc. could be made, appear in our consciousness as very base; by contrast the investigations which have no specific use at all here seem to be for the definite and higher aim. It would thus be not only useless, but also absurd to raise their powers above their purpose, aim, and use. Accordingly another life must be being kept for us where this has its aim and its use. Furthermore, the sciences and speculations require that a part of humanity work more so that another part has more time and leisure for speculating, and must not worry about means of acquisition or nourishment. But if now there were no other destiny; then this inequality amongst humans would be very incommensurate with this life. Indeed the human who leans on sciences and speculations puts many advantages of this life to the side; he shortens his life and weakens his health. Since thus suchlike sciences are not at all fitting for our present destiny; they must be in anticipation of another destiny where they will have more value. Furthermore the shortness of human life does not suffice for making *use* of all the sciences and knowledge which you have acquired. Life is too short to develop your talents fully. When you have brought it to the highest level in the sciences and now would like to make the best use of it, then you die. If, for example, a Newton had lived longer; then he alone would have invented more than all humans together would not have invented in a thousand years. Only when he had brought it to the highest level in the sciences, he died. After him comes again someone who must begin from the A B C, and when he has brought it just as far, then he too dies; and with the following one it goes just the same. Accordingly the shortness of life has no proportion at all to the talent of the human understanding. Since now nothing in nature is in vain; this must also be preserved for another life. *The sciences are the luxury of understanding which gives us a foretaste of that which we will be in the future life.*

If we consider on the other hand the powers of the will; we find a mainspring for morality and uprightness in us. Should this be made for us merely in this life; then nature has the best of us. All of it would be useless if the soul were to have no further extent to its destiny. Supposing another being, a spirit, came to earth, and it were to see a pregnant woman open in whose body another being was. It would see further that this being would have organs which it could not, however, at all use in the state in which it finds itself; then this spirit would have to conclude necessarily that the being was being kept for another state in which it will be able to use all its organs. And we ourselves even conclude thus; when we, for example, see a caterpillar, and become aware that it already has all the organs which it will need afterwards as a butterfly — that it will make use of them according to its development. Likewise the soul of the human is equipped with powers of knowledge and desire, with drives and moral feeling, which have no sufficient purpose for this life. Since now nothing is in vain, but rather everything has its aim; these abilities of the soul must also have their specific aim. Because now this does not arrive in the present life; it must then be kept for a future life.

The difficulty which accompanies this proof rests on the following reproach: the procreation of humans is incidental; it rests always upon the human, whether they want to set themselves in the state for producing children or not; it rests merely on their inclination, on their idea. Often even children are produced in an impermissible way, when persons meet one another in a great heat. Humans here could thus be put to stud just as well as other animals. Now no creature which is placed by birth into the world by means of the accidental decision of its parents can be destined for a higher aim and a future life. It is indeed true, if the humans would otherwise not at all have come into life except through the aim of animal birth, which is very accidental; then this would be not just a perfect objection, but rather even a proof. Only we see on the other hand that the life of the soul does not rest on the accidental nature of the breeding of animal life; but rather that it has already lasted *before* the animal life, and thus its existence depends on a higher purpose. The *animal life is consequently incidental, but the spiritual is not*. The spiritual life could though persist and be exercised even if it were also united accidentally with the body. If the beings which have not been born, or cannot have been born, were not equally blessed with human life; then indeed this spirit which would then have been developed through the shell of a body can be developed though in a different way. Even if this answer to the objection does not yet fully prove the matter; it is of so much use that the objection to which it is opposed does not apply, and we are thus secured in our belief of assuming a future life.

As to what concerns the nature of the state of the soul on the other side of the boundary of life, we will not be able to say here anything reliably in that the limits of our reason stretch up to the boundary, but do not go beyond it. — Accordingly only concepts will occur which can be opposed to the objections being made. Firstly it is to be asked whether the soul in its future state will be conscious of itself, or not. — If it were not conscious of itself; then this would be the *spiritual death* which we have refuted already through the foregoing concepts. But if it is not conscious whether its life power is still the same there; then this is the *spiritual slumber* in which the soul does not know where it is, and cannot yet reconcile itself properly to the other world. The same lack of life power and of consciousness, however, cannot be proven at all; for because the soul is itself the life power, it cannot have any lack of it.

The *personality*, the main thing with the soul after the death, and the identity of the personality of the soul, however, consists in that it is conscious that it is a person, and that it is also conscious of its identity; for otherwise the previous state would not be connected with the future state at all. The personality can be taken *practically* and *psychologically*; *practically* when free actions are ascribed to it; *psychologically* when it is conscious of itself and its identity. The consciousness of itself and the identity of the person rests on the inner mind. The inner mind, however, also still remains though without the body because the body is not a principle of life, thus too the personality.

But if now the soul is conscious of itself; then it is to be asked: is it conscious of itself *as a pure spirit, or connected with an organic body*? Of this we cannot say anything reliable. There are two sorts of opinions over this:

1) You can either imagine a restitution of the animal life, which can be either of an earthly or of a supernatural sort. According to the earthly sort, my soul would have to assume this or another body; according to the supernatural sort, which would be a transition out of this life into another animal life, the soul would have to assume a transfigured body. Or you could also think of:

2) an entirely pure spiritual life, where the soul will have no body at all.

This last opinion is the most appropriate for philosophy. For if the body is a hindrance to life, but the future body should be perfect, then it must be *fully spiritual*. If we now, however, assume a fully spiritual life; then you can ask here again: where is heaven? Where is hell? And which is our future destination? The separation of the soul from the body is not to be set in a change of place. The presence of the spirit cannot be explained locally. For if it is explained locally; then I can, when the human is dead, ask: does the soul still sit for a long time in the body? Or does it go from it straightaway? Is it accordingly in the room or in the house? And how long may it surely spend on its journey, be it to heaven or to hell? Or where is it otherwise? All these questions, however, fall away when you do not assume and explain the presence of the spirit locally. Places are only circumstances of corporeal things, but not of spiritual things. Accordingly the soul, because it takes up no space, is not to be seen in the entire corporeal world; it has no specific place in the corporeal world, but rather it is in the spirit world; it stands in connection and in relationship with other spirits. If now these spirits are benevolent and sacred beings, and the soul is in their community; then it is *in heaven*. When the community of spirits in which it finds itself, however, is malignant; then the soul is *in hell. Heaven is thus everywhere such a community of sacred spiritual beings is*; it is, however, nowhere, because it takes up no place in the world, in that the community is not erected in the corporeal world. Accordingly heaven will not be the immeasurable space which the world bodies take up, and which shows itself in the colour blue where you would have to travel up into the air if you want to arrive there*; but rather heaven is the spirit world; and to stand in relationship to and in communion with the spirit world means *to be in heaven*. Accordingly the soul will not arrive in hell if it has been malicious; but rather it will just see itself in the society of evil spirits, and that means *being in hell. —*

We have a knowledge of the corporeal world through our sensory view to the extent it appears to us; our consciousness is made to act as an astringent to the animal view; the present world is the *commercium* of all objects to the extent they are seen through present sensory view. But if the soul parts from the body; then it will not view the world as it appears, but rather as it is. Accordingly the separation of the soul from the body consists in the *change of the sensory view into the spiritual view; and that is the other world*. The other world is accordingly not another place, but rather just another view. The other world remains with respect to the objects the same world; it is not distinguished according to the substances; only it is *viewed spiritually*. Those who imagine the other world as if it were a *new place* which was isolated from this one, and to which you must only be transported if you want to arrive there; they must then also take the separation of the soul locally and explain its presence locally. Then its presence

---

*   [Tr.: note that the German words for heaven and sky are the same word.]

78

would rest on corporeal conditions, as on the contact, extension in space, etc.; but then many questions would also occur, and you would descend into materialism. But since the presence of the soul is spiritual; the separation must not consist in the departing of the soul from the body, and in the going into another world; but rather since the soul has through the body a view of the corporeal world; it will then, if it is freed from the sensory view of the body, have a spiritual view, and that is the other world. When you arrive in the other world; then you do not arrive in a community of other things, say on other planets; for with them I am already in connection, even if only in a more distant way; but rather you remain in this world, but have a spiritual view of everything. Thus the other world is not distinguished according to place from this one; the concept of place cannot be used here at all. Accordingly the state of blessedness, or of heaven, and the state of misery, or of hell, all of which the other world holds within itself, also does not have to be sought in this sensory world; but rather if I have been righteous here, and after death receive a spiritual view of everything, and enter into the community of just such righteous beings; then I am in heaven. But if I receive according to my behaviour a spiritual view of such beings whose wills stand at cross purposes to all the rules of morality, and if I end up in such a community; then I am in hell. Indeed this opinion of the other world cannot be demonstrated, but it is a necessary hypothesis of reason.

The thought of Swedenborg is quite sublime here. He says: the spirit world comprises a special real universe; this is the *mundus intelligibilis* [intelligible world] which must be distinguished from this *mundo sensibili* [perceivable world]. He says: all spiritual natures stand in connection with one another; only the communion and connection to the spirits is not tied to the condition of the body; there not one spirit is far or near from the others, but rather it is a spiritual connection. Now our souls stand as spirits in this connection and in communion with one another, and indeed often here in this world; only we do not see ourselves in this community because we still have a sensory outlook; but although we do not see ourselves in it, we do stand in it anyway. If now the hindrance to the spiritual view is once raised; then we will see ourselves in this spiritual community, and this is the other world; now this is not other things, but rather the same things which we are viewing, however, differently. If now a human has been righteous in the world, whose will is a well-disposed will, who makes an effort to exercise the rules of morality; he is in this world already in communion with all righteous and well-disposed souls, be they in India or in Arabia; only he will not yet see himself in this community until he is freed from the sensory outlook. Likewise the malicious person is also already here in the community of all malignants who detest each other mutually; only he does not yet see himself in it. But when he is freed from his sensory outlook; then he becomes aware of himself in it. Accordingly every good act of the virtuous is a step towards the community of the blessed, just as every evil act is a step towards the community of the depraved. Accordingly the virtuous one does not arrive in heaven, but rather he is already in it here; but after the death he will see himself for the first time in this community. Likewise the malicious cannot see themselves in hell, although they are already really in it. But when they are freed from the body; then they will see for the first time where they are. Terrible thoughts for the malignant! Does he not have to fear every moment that his spiritual eyes will be opened? And as soon as these open, he is already in hell.

How the body should be necessary for this spiritual view, I do not understand at all. Why should the soul still be surrounded with this dust, when it is once freed of it? This is all that we can say here in order to clarify the concept of the spiritual nature of the soul, of its separation from the body, and of the future world which consists in heaven and hell. —

To conclude the psychology *the spirits absolutely* should still be examined; of them we can, however, not understand anything more through our reason *than that such spirits are possible.*

Only one question remains yet: whether the soul, which sees itself already spiritually in the other world, will and can appear in the visible world through visible effects. This is *not possible*; for matter can only be experienced sensorially and fall on the external senses, but a spirit cannot. Or could I not already to some extent *view here* the community of parted souls with my soul which is not yet parted, but which stands in communion with them as a spirit? For example, like Swedenborg will? This is contradictory; for then the spiritual view must already begin in this world. But since I still have a sensory view in this world; *I cannot at the same time have a spiritual view*. I cannot be at the same time in this and also in that world; for if I have a sensory view; then I am in this, and if I have a spiritual view, then I am in the other world; but this cannot occur at the same time. Given, however, it were possible that the soul could still appear in this world, or that such a spiritual view were already possible here, in that we cannot though prove the impossibility of it; then here the maxim of sound reason must be opposed. But the maxim of sound reason is this: *to not allow, but rather to reject all such experiences and phenomena which are such that, if I assume them, they make the use of my reason impossible, and annul the conditions under which my reason can alone be used*. Were this to be assumed; then the use of my reason would cease altogether in this world; *then many actions could occur on account of the spirits*. However this needs no closer consideration, since you see from experience that, if a malefactor shoves the guilt for his actions on an evil spirit which is supposed to have led him to it, the judge does not let this apply as an excuse. For otherwise he also would not be able to punish such a man.

In general we offer *that it is not appropriate at all here for our destiny to worry much about the future world; but rather we must complete the circle to which we are destined here and wait to see how it will be in respect to the future world*. The main thing is that we behave in this position righteously and morally good, and seek to make ourselves worthy of future fortune. Just like it would be illogical if you occupied the lowest position in the military and worried about the state of the colonel or general. It is only time for that when you arrive at it.

Providence has occluded from us the future world, and left us only a small hope which is sufficient enough to move us to make *ourselves worthy of it*; which we would not do so eagerly if we already knew the future world exactly ahead of time.

The main thing is always morality; this is the sacred and inviolable thing which we must protect, and this is also the basis and the aim of all our speculations and investigations. All metaphysical speculations lead from it. *God* and the *other world* is the only goal of all our philosophical investigations, and if the concepts of God and of the other world are not connected with morality, then they are of no use.

***